STEFANIE POWERS: SUPERLIFE!

By Stefanie Powers
and JUDY QUINE

Photography by Rob Lewine

SIMON AND SCHUSTER
NEW YORK

Copyright © 1985 by Yoakum Valley Productions, and Balaban & Quine, Inc.
All rights reserved
including the right of reproduction
in whole or in part in any form
Published by Simon and Schuster
A Division of Simon & Schuster, Inc.
Simon & Schuster Building
Rockefeller Center
1230 Avenue of the Americas
New York, New York 10020
SIMON AND SCHUSTER and colophon are registered trademarks of Simon & Schuster, Inc.
Designed by Elizabeth Woll
Manufactured in the United States of America

10   9   8   7   6   5   4   3   2   1

Library of Congress Cataloging in Publication Data

Powers, Stefanie.
  Stefanie Powers: Superlife!

  1.Exercise for women.   2.Karate.   3.Physical
fitness for women.   I.Quine, Judy.   II.Title.
III.Title: Stephanie Powers: Superlife!
GV482.P64   1985   613.7′045   84-22182

ISBN: 0-671-50616-1

ACKNOWLEDGMENTS

A great many people gave of their time, energy, talent and wisdom to help us during the writing of this book. We particularly want to thank Ellen Sklarz, Rob Lewine, Bill Wallace, Ernie Reyes, Sr., and Ernie Reyes, Jr., as they each made valuable and generous contributions. We also express our gratitude to Don Quine, PKA President; Joe Corley, PKA Executive Vice President, and John Worley and Pat Roufus, Members of the PKA Executive Committee. Additionally we thank Paul Vizzio, PKA Featherweight World Champion, for his insight with regard to kata, and for providing us with a living example of ying/yang at its best. Elsworth F. Baker, M.D., President of the American College of Orgonomy and author of *Man in the Trap*, provided us with valuable guidance, as did our friends and coworkers at Simon and Schuster, Dan Green and Susan Victor. Our thanks also to Diana Reynolds, Yuki, Jann Rowe, Sherri Clayton, Annie Gilbar and Carol Greenstein; to Eugene Carl Webb, Doctor of Chiropractic; to Anna Cheselko and Alex Rodine of the Anna Cheselko Dance Center; to Bernie Krasnoo of the Sherman Oaks Karate Studio and to Phyla and John Davidson of the Taoist Chinese Internal System. We are, as always, most grateful for the love and support of Mama Julie, Amy, Vicki, Nina, Robert, James and Sean.

We lovingly dedicate this book
to those who believe
that the process of life is its own reward.

PREFACE

Dear Readers,

In this book, you will find a combination of old and new ideas, redefined to communicate some of the things Judy Quine and I feel are essential components of the sort of healthy mind and body that produces the glow of self-confidence.

It is no coincidence that when we feel good we look good; and feeling good has everything to do with the body we walk around in and the mind and spirit that move it. Thus, to realize our full potential, we cannot help but address ourselves to all three aspects.

I have long been fascinated by the ancient disciplines of karate and yoga which unite the mind, body and spirit to achieve the condition of total well-being. But not all of us wish to be a yoga or a Black Belt. In developing the Superlife System, Judy and I looked for those elements of exercise that provide a personal sense of accomplishment and gratification.

In reality, there is "nothing new under the sun," so no doubt you will recognize some of the exercises in this book, but perhaps you never thought of combining them in quite the same way, or internalizing the feelings that make them a part of you. That is what we hope this book will become—a part of you, inspired by a part of us.

ENJOY!

CONTENTS

PART I

INTRODUCTION TO SUPERLIFE

THE AUTHORS

We, Stefanie Powers and Judy Quine, are friends who lead very different lives. One of us is single and an actress; the other is a sports executive, married, with six children and two grandchildren.

STEFANIE POWERS

For the past six years, my role as Jennifer Hart on the television series "Hart to Hart" has necessitated fourteen-hour days, five days a week, for nine and a half months a year. My career has spanned twenty-four years, but it has been the success of "Hart to Hart" that has brought the opportunity to expand my horizons professionally and has opened the doors to the realization of some of my personal dreams.

With the establishment of my own production company, Karoger Productions, and the release in 1984 of *Family Secrets*, the first of six properties I have written for the company, some of my professional goals are beginning to fall into place.

Another goal involves a great deal of work as president of the William Holden Wildlife Foundation, formed in order that the principles of Bill's work and ideas could be carried on. The foundation is now in the process of building the Wildlife Education Center in Kenya, offering a curriculum that pro-

Judy and her family

vides alternatives to the slaughter of wildlife and destruction of the land.

The foundation's dreams will never be fulfilled entirely in my lifetime, but we can get a good start toward achieving something beyond any one individual's existence. This life's work offers me the chance to give back to the world something of value and is a way of showing my gratitude for the many blessings I have been afforded.

One of my other great satisfactions in life is travel. From my earliest days, the lust for travel and the experiencing of foreign lands and people have been such passions for me that I consider them to be integral parts of my being.

I do not travel frivolously; it is more an occupation. Before and during a visit to any country, I study to learn all I can about the history, culture and current concerns of that nation and its people.

Some of this may have practical applications now that I have established a production company. Assuredly, all of it has increased my understanding of the human condition.

I am not, however, simply a wanderer. I also love my home, family, friends, pets and my involvement in sports—especially those that include a horse or two. But the one thing I value over and above all else is health in mind, body and spirit.

JUDY QUINE

Ten years ago, my husband, Don Quine, and I cofounded the Professional Karate Association (PKA). Both Don and I had been previously married, and together we raised six children from our prior marriages.

The PKA became our seventh child. To found a new professional sport and build it in this era, our workdays—then and now—would range from ten to seventeen hours, five to seven days a week. This work schedule—particularly when all the children were younger—meant we had to make do with almost no adult social life. Fortunately, friends have been both patient and faithful. And as the children grew up, we resumed, as though without interruption, old friendships and made new ones as well.

During that same period, I served on the board of trustees of my children's school, as well as on the boards of the American Civil Liberties Union Foundation of Southern California and other organizations whose work concerns me greatly. In 1977, I was appointed a commissioner of a large regulatory agency of the state of California. I chaired that board for a time and am still serving on it as one of thirteen commissioners.

I travel frequently, to wherever my work takes me—throughout California for state responsibilities and around the United States and to Europe for PKA business. When the children were younger they often traveled with me. Now that they are older, some with their own children, we travel together less, but the family still spends an enormous amount of time together.

I was born and raised in the entertainment world. For more than twenty-five years my father was president of Paramount Pictures. Nothing in my background influenced me to work in sports or in government. Unlike Stefanie, I had not been an active participant in sports since I abandoned my field hockey and lacrosse sticks on my high school playing field at the end of the 1940s.

My interests are extremely eclectic, and I thoroughly enjoy pursuing them fully. Fortunately, I have been blessed with good physical health, an active mind and a large appetite for challenges. To maintain and regenerate my well-being, I have learned it is essential to make an investment in it as is the case with everything else in life.

THE PKA

The PKA—the Professional Karate Association—was founded in 1974. Its original purpose was to create, regulate and build a new, professional sport: contact karate. This sport is now seen on NBC and ESPN television more than two hundred hours each year.

Karate is a two-thousand-year-old discipline in which actual contact is not permitted during matches. Contact karate—an evolution from that original base—involves sports competition in which full-contact hand and foot moves are made by the athletes.

In creating the new sport, the best elements of various karate styles were utilized. Almost everyone who became a part of the PKA brought with him or her a high sense of respect, discipline and a dedication to a common goal: the growth of

Practicing kicks with PKA Kata
Champions, Ernie Reyes Senior and
Junior

the new sport. They also brought an unwavering sense of purpose to maintain high safety standards for its athletes. Perhaps that is why no contact-karate athlete has suffered a death or a serious injury in more than thirteen thousand one-on-one matches.

As the sport of contact karate grew, so did the number of men, women and children who studied karate in its non-contact form, for fitness and self-confidence. More than fifteen million people now study exercise karate in schools and classes held everywhere in the United States. It is taught in karate schools, colleges and universities, community Y's and recreation centers. Churches and synagogues hold classes, as do health clubs and spas; and the athletes of many major league teams in most professional sports study it.

As Judy traveled to karate schools and student tournaments throughout the U.S., women told her about their increased ability to balance family and work responsibilities more readily. They told her that karate exercise had helped them feel more confident, improved their relationships and helped them move ahead more assertively in the business world. Men told her that karate helped them in every aspect of their lives, enabling them to become more involved fathers, more supportive husbands and to focus on their career goals more accurately.

Children who had been painfully shy told how karate training had helped them come out of their shells. Those with bad grades commented on the improvement in their schoolwork. And parents of adolescents described how karate had helped pull their teenagers out of the boredom that was leading in the direction of drug or alcohol abuse.

Everyone spoke of more self-confidence.

In 1983, Don Quine (PKA president) and Judy (PKA executive board chairperson) began to develop an instructional version of the PKA Superlife System for the Presidential Sports Fitness Program. They worked with the most noted karate experts as well as with a variety of doctors in the fitness field.

The President's Council on Physical Fitness and Sports conducts several programs designed to motivate people throughout the country toward healthier life-styles. Presidential Sports Fitness Awards are granted to those individuals who spend a minimum of fifty hours in one of forty-two different physical activities during the program year. There are Presidential Corporate Fitness Programs and Presidential Sports Fitness

Festivals conducted in cities throughout the United States.

In 1984, I had the honor of serving as a national spokesperson for the Presidential Sports Fitness Program. It was the year after karate had become part of that program's activities. My friend Bill Wallace, retired PKA World Middleweight Champion and a karate legend, was also a national spokesperson that same year.

HOW JUDY AND I CAME TO SUPERLIFE

I needed one all-encompassing exercise program that satisfied my physical, mental and emotional needs. One regimen would offer a particular conditioning benefit for my body; another would give me a better approach to meditation. At one point, I found myself trying to do five separate programs simultaneously—and unsuccessfully—simply because I could not spend the whole day at home or running off to classes. I don't know of many women who have the time to be program "junkies." Most of us are too busy trying to organize and live our lives.

Feeling guilty about not putting the necessary time into each endeavor, I stopped all of them. The truth is that after I stopped exercising, I didn't feel as well, didn't look as well, and found my energy level dropping far below normal. During that same period, while shooting "Hart to Hart," I organized a large fundraising benefit for the Wildlife Foundation. I was also writing, producing and acting in my own TV movie.

I knew I needed to be involved with some kind of health/fitness/beauty regimen, but I had to be very clear about exactly what I wanted most from a program that could be done effectively in the limited time I had available. I realized I was long past the age of winning an Olympic track-and-field medal and that what I was most concerned with was being able to maintain an overall stability of mind, body and spirit that would accompany me throughout my life.

Just at that time, my friend Judy Quine dropped in to visit. Judy told me that she had become more and more neglectful—as the years passed—about doing anything with regard to physical exercise. "I've used every classic excuse for why I can't exercise regularly—too much work, too much travel, too many other people depending on me," she said. "If I

stopped to jog, meditate, do aerobics and lift weights, I'd have to retire from general living."

While helping to develop PKA Superlife as an instructional system for the Presidential Sports Fitness Program, Judy had suddenly realized that right under her nose was an ideal, do-it-at-home mind/body/spirit exercise system. It satisfied all her requirements, which are quite similar to my own.

As we talked, I recalled the time I had spent studying karate and tai chi. There had, indeed, been facets of those workouts that had come close to fulfilling my own needs. As Judy described the PKA Superlife System to me, I could see she was distilling the best of those disciplines I had studied and combining them with other elements to form a program that could easily be wedded to my own life.

So Judy and I decided to work together to develop a home version of Superlife, one that could be done without studio instruction, one to which we could lend our own personal insights.

Using ourselves as guinea pig practitioners, we modified certain techniques, selecting them from one style or the other. We met with PKA athletes and trainers, and tested each segment of the system for the amount of workout time required. We examined what parts of the Superlife philosophy were directly applicable to the physical moves, and how the two—practiced together—made us feel.

Everywhere we went, we spoke with friends and acquaintances about what we were doing. All of them—whether they worked out or not—told us what they wanted most was exactly what we were looking for: a "package deal" for their well-being, their looks, the enhancement of their lives.

Like us, they all wanted it to be practical in terms of time. They also wanted elements of the system they could use anywhere—at home, at the office, on the road—wherever they needed a moment or more of relaxation, strength or confidence.

WHY KARATE?

Why, in the middle of the 1980s, should Americans be attracted to an exercise system that began thousands of years ago in the Orient? And why, specifically, should this attraction focus on the Eastern martial art of karate?

The answer lies in the fact that Americans like to get the job at hand done, done well and done in the shortest possible amount of time.

So, let's first identify the job at hand—what most of us want and expect of an exercise system. Perhaps I'm greedy, but I want it to help me create my *total* self as I wish to be, and I suspect that's what you are after too.

We all want well-shaped, well-toned bodies, but I believe we also want strong and focused minds along with positive attitudes to put the most into our daily lives and get the most back from them. We all want to feel that we are full of personal power and self-confidence, that we look well, feel well and can move with purpose and success toward our various personal and professional goals.

The Eastern exercise system of karate, and specifically Superlife with its visualization and key breathing techniques and its physical movements, provides the method for evolving your total self into the person you want to be. It is a practical system, one you can utilize constantly in every facet of your daily life.

Superlife embodies techniques and methods for seeing yourself as you wish to be and for becoming that person.

YIN AND YANG

Karate embraces the wisdom of yin and yang—the feminine and masculine in every person, in every aspect of life.

Reviewing Phase One construction of the William Holden Wildlife Education Center, completed in May 1984.

The son of Kenya's Minister of Wildlife and Tourism visits a favorite
cheetah with me.

The possibilities and options in women's lives today make many of us feel we are being asked to become superwomen (as we incorporate the masculine yang into our lives). "Take care of your face. Take care of your body. Take care of your family, your house, your job, your community." These demands are enormous and unending.

I like being a woman. I treasure those qualities I associate with womanliness—such as intuitiveness, grace and generosity of spirit. But I also value my right to satisfy my curiosity about the world as well as the freedom today's life-style offers to help me realize my ambitions.

It is not an easy time for anyone; transitions are always difficult. Old orders need to be replaced with new ones. But this era has prospects for everyone's growth and fulfillment. Perhaps that is what Pierre Teilhard de Chardin meant in *The Phenomenon of Man*, where he wrote: "There is for us in the future not only survival but superlife."

The future Teilhard de Chardin was speaking about is now. And in order to enhance our lives, we need to redefine some of life's important elements.

HEALTH AND WELL-BEING

When we first started writing this book, Judy and I looked up the word "health" in the 1977 edition of *Webster's*. It defined the word as "the condition of being sound in mind, body or spirit." But we think of a person as being healthy, not as either/ or but as a whole person. Don't you? Doesn't each of us know someone who has no specific mental illness nor any disease but who is too often painfully depressed or negative? Do you think of that person as healthy? Or do you, like us, see the person's whole well-being?

The 1982 revision of *Webster's* has taken out the "or," added an "and," and begun to identify the matter of health as a unit, rather than as separate fragments. One never knows whether society catches up to the dictionary, or whether the dictionary catches up to us. Even women's fashion magazines blaze such headlines at us as: "New Definition of Fitness: A Healthy Mind/Body Attitude" (*Vogue* magazine, November 1983). We know that such publications reflect what we are thinking and doing.

Well-being, however, is the flourishing of every bit of

thought, feeling, energy and action you invest into your life. It is not simply your face and body; nor your intelligence, courage and character. It is not merely your personality, accomplishments and sense of humor; nor just your relationships with friends, family and coworkers. Your well-being encompasses all of that—and more.

We live in an age of specialization. People are classified according to their skills in the work force. This fragmenting concept is applied to both the individual and to humanity in general.

However, it is not largely held that this notion doesn't work when applied to the *whole* individual. If I do not perceive myself as a unified entity called *me*, it is extremely difficult for *me* to feel really connected either to the universe or to the life I lead. The age of specialization has made many of us feel isolated, disenfranchised—detached from the central thread of life.

Dozens of specialists have invented hundreds of ways to work on the thousand and one elements that make up our personas, as if we were a society composed of Humpty Dumpties, waiting—in pieces—for all the king's men to put us back together again.

But we are not machines. We cannot send a part of ourselves out to be fixed. All of our parts are related and contained in one human package.

Thus, in recent years, the idea of developing our whole well-beings began to become more prominent. These ideas—based primarily on the interrelationship between our attitudes, our health and our looks—are now heard and practiced everywhere. We read about them in fashion and sports magazines. We hear about them from professionals in the health care field. Our friends discuss them at dinner.

This newly prevalent attitude is referred to as a holistic (or "whole-istic") approach to well-being. This approach seems to be helping people to live better and longer lives and is being studied and utilized throughout the world in doctors' offices and hospitals, by insurance companies and government health plans.

Actually, "holistic" means emphasizing the organic and functional relationships between parts and wholes. I've found it to be the most valid, applicable concept for pursuing my own well-being.

EXERCISE

According to its familiar meaning, "exercise" entails organized bodily movement that helps to keep us physically fit. But to me, exercise entails putting all parts of myself into active use in a specific manner. True, most exercises can take my mind off everyday concerns, but even when I complete a strenuous exercise routine, the concerns come right back and I still have to deal with them. My body may feel energized and conditioned, but I have not received any particular indication that my brain is sharper than it was before working out. Nor have I been able to identify quite how my spirit might have been reinforced the better to cope with the day's challenges.

When I work out, I want to know exactly how I am supposed to feel in order to know if I am doing each exercise correctly.

I also want a specific focus for my mind, a clear image in my mind's eye that helps me to work my mental reflexes along with those of my body.

But what about that good old ephemeral spirit? Can it actually be exercised? Absolutely! "Spirit" describes our dispositions, our sensitivities, how we feel about ourselves and life, what we have faith in. It is as real a part of ourselves as our minds and bodies.

For centuries we were told that mind, body and spirit were all separate entities, not interactive parts of one whole. The notion was that thought was in the mind, that it was abstracted and isolated in the brain. As for feelings, they came from the heart, the "gut" or some unknown part of the body. They were not abstracted but were, we perceived, lively and intense. For

a long time, psychiatry confirmed this belief in the separation between thoughts and feelings. Whatever one might think, early psychiatrists told us, our unconscious would dictate how we really felt.

Today, though, many psychiatrists, endocrinologists and neurobiologists are saying that thoughts and feelings may be produced in the same part of the body. Or perhaps, they say, the body uses the identical method to produce thoughts and feelings—maybe even the same chemical components. These medical professionals, along with many others, acknowledge that our feelings, our thoughts and our bodies are all inter-related and often interactive. For this reason, the Superlife System contains specific approaches for working on all three personal elements.

BEAUTY

The word "beauty" is being redefined everywhere. We once thought of beauty as how bones and features were assembled on a particular face and body. We placed an inordinately high value on the accident by which some people were, in those limited terms, beautiful. We idealized our beauties, the ones the world acknowledged as having the exemplary face or form—the face everyone else wanted to possess, the body we looked upon as perfection.

We know now that that definition did not work well for most of us. There was a period of years (I was just coming into womanhood) when everyone wanted to look like Marilyn Monroe. It is obvious that even with a lifetime of reconstructive surgery, I would never come close. Tragically we discovered that looking like Marilyn Monroe was not enough—even for her.

At the height of Marilyn's stardom, Judy accompanied her to a glamorous, New York movie première. Thousands of screaming fans lined the two women's way to the postpremière party, pushing, shoving, reaching out to try to touch Marilyn. Reporters, photographers and fans were caught in half-closed elevator doors in an attempt to be with her for the ride to the rooftop ballroom.

As Marilyn and Judy made their way to the ladies' room, dozens of other fans were knocked over, trampled in the crush. Once inside, they went to the mirror to touch up their makeup.

As they both faced the looking glass, Marilyn said to Judy, "My face, my body . . . they're an accident. I didn't make them. I can only tinker with them. Even then, they'll fall apart. It isn't much, is it?"

It has taken quite a while, but at last the time is upon us when we have redefined "beauty" to include much more of ourselves. Even mainstream purveyors of beauty tell us about the change. A *Vogue* magazine headline (August 1983) said: "Great Looks Now: More Than Just a Pretty Face . . . Real Spirit . . . Vitality . . . Knockout Energy . . . Glowing, Healthy Appeal. It's a whole new definition of beauty, one that owes more to a woman's attitude than ever before."

And the dictionary has really done it! It now defines "beauty" as "the quality attributed to whatever pleases or satisfies the senses or mind, as by line, color, form, texture, proportion, rhythmic motion, tone, etc., or by behavior, attitude, etc." Way to go *Webster's*!

An era in which we are free to define things in an entirely new way cannot be anything other than exciting. Our imaginations, our curiosities are stimulated. We feel energized, encouraged, enthusiastic about the possibilities we can discover to make our lives fuller and better. We are no longer tied to definitions of qualities that may, forever, elude us.

It is wonderful to know that our eyes don't have to be Elizabeth Taylor's to be beautiful. They merely need to be warm and alert, and expressive of our own selves. And it is such a relief to realize that so many great bodies are not measured by a single set of inches and proportions we may never achieve.

Now the measure of a great body is judged by its sense of vigor, conditioning, toning and a positive attitude about the way we move through our lives. It is exhilarating to think that we can define our own goals—whatever they may be—rather than having to settle on a limited set of goals dictated by an unknown group called "they."

POWER

Judy and I wish to be very clear about our intent. The primary purpose of encouraging you to work the PKA Superlife System is to make you as powerful as you can be. Because the matter

of each individual's personal power is so vital to us, we would like to reexamine what power is all about.

For two or more decades, "power" was a buzzword, one with a rather ugly connotation. Powerful persons were those who manipulated the lives of others solely for the benefit of the powerful. Powerful people seemed mindless about how the abuses of power might affect the individual or society. The powerful were selfish, had an unending appetite for wealth and a perverse desire to intimidate others in order to satisfy their own ego needs. Who would admit, openly, to wanting power of that sort?

Now, however, in a time when we are free to redefine such words as health, beauty and exercise, it is well worth redefining power to take a fresh look at its productive possibilities.

Webster's lists fourteen definitions of the word "power." Fear not, we won't include them all here! But do take a look at a few of those words and phrases: "the ability to do, act or produce"; "a specific ability or faculty"; "...vigor..."; "a source of...energy"; "a person...having great influence, force or authority." Is there any one of us who would wish to be without power? We think not.

Can power be acquired or increased? Or is it some mysterious element you are either born with or doomed to live without forever? We believe the former. And is power one specific tool? Or is it an amalgamation of tools that produces an aura based on your own self-image, as well as on how others perceive you? We say the latter.

In our terms, power is each person's ability to manage his or her own life with a strong sense of personal freedom that carries with it an equally strong sense of responsibility. We place an extraordinarily high value on that kind of power.

Most of us were told that when we became adults, we would not only have more freedom but also the responsibilities that go along with it. For many of us, the notion of freedom held a bonus of pleasure, while the idea of its accompanying responsibilities were the adult burden we had to bear. A number of us, particularly women, were victims of the Cinderella responsibility-free myth, the one that told us: If we cleaned up others' messes and kept our mouths shut, we would one day be blessed by a fairy godmother, rescued by a handsome prince, relieved of all our responsibilities and freed to live happily ever after (presumably dumping our responsibilities on some other poor soul not yet scheduled for a visit from her fairy godmother).

But the truth is that freedom and responsibilities are all tied up in one package and are the reward for being a grown-up. When we feel strong and confident about meeting our responsibilities, we feel relaxed and take pleasure in treating ourselves to our freedoms.

The amalgamated elements of personal power can be found in the Superlife Guidelines. When you communicate clearly and creatively, breathe properly, visualize productively, stretch yourself, stay flexible, maintain clear focus in thought, attitude and action; when you have a strong center, keen balance, are able to relax and manage stress effectively, and feel both self-respect as well as respect for others, you have all the power you need for a superlife. From experience, Judy and I can tell you that when you feel you have that kind of power, others feel you do too.

PART II

GUIDELINES
Working the Superlife System

KEY BREATHING

Every exercise book we have ever read, and the instructor in every class we have ever attended, has told us to breathe while we exercise. But nobody has ever explained how to breathe properly. Nor has anyone told us how important, even crucial, proper breathing is in *all* moments of our lives—whether we are exercising or not.

Later, in Part III of the book, you will learn the techniques of key breathing. Here we want you to become conscious about it and to realize just how vital it is to your general well-being.

The term "key breathing" evolved from a number of sources, all of which stress breathing as the key to your life force. In the various Chinese systems of exercise, it is called *chi* ("chee")—"inherent energy." It can also be called the "mind/body/spirit force of blood and breath"; or it can simply refer to the air that moves in, out of and through our bodies during respiration.

Tai chi is the slow-motion exercise system practiced by millions of Chinese in every walk of life. *Tai* comes from the *Tao*, a book of poems reputedly written during the fourth century B.C. The *Tao* deals with the ultimate natural order of universal reality, and sets forth the goal of living life in harmony with that order. Thus tai chi means the activity that reinforces both our perception of the universe and our place

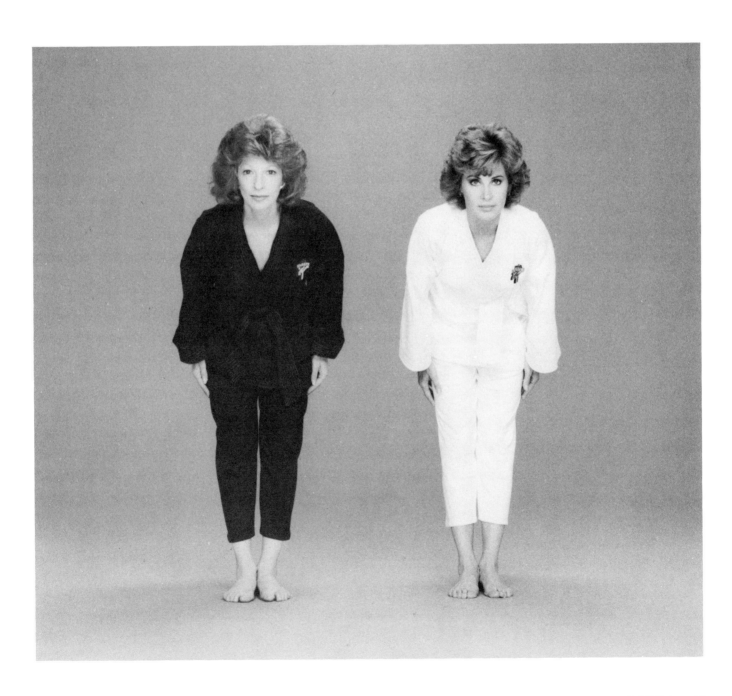

within it, and our ability to maintain well-being of mind/body/spirit.

The Japanese-language version of the Chinese *chi* breath element is called *ki* ("key"). It is the source of the *ki-ai* (pronounced "key-eye"), the sounds made by people when they practice karate. These focused sounds—and particularly the breath that accompanies them—are believed to be the source of one's "super power." Though this may sound mystical, it is a technique we have all utilized. Haven't we all tried to lift, push or pull something that seems too heavy to move? At the moment we feel it is impossible don't we unconsciously emit a gruntlike sound? And doesn't the very making of that sound and the breath expended to create it furnish us with the final spurt of energy needed to get the job done? That is the principle of *ki-ai*.

Both Eastern cultures acknowledge breath as one of the primary elements of well-being, and both teach specific methods of correct breathing. In the United States, however, we did not hear much about breath until the advent of the fitness boom.

We know now that certain repeated movements made at a given rate of speed during physical exercise raise the rate at which we take in oxygen and increase the amount of oxygen intake. As strenuously working muscles (including the heart) demand more oxygen, the cardiovascular system is called upon to meet that demand. Any system of exercise (including running, swimming, karate and others) that increases and sustains the activity of the cardiovascular system during a twenty-to-thirty-minute workout period is, by definition, an aerobic exercise.

Other than our recent information on aerobic conditioning, most of us know only those few basic facts we learned in school. We inhale and take oxygen into our lungs. We exhale and let out carbon dioxide. The oxygen is carried through the body via a network of arteries and capillaries; carbon dioxide is carried away by the veins.

The key fact we seem to ignore is that once the oxygen enters our lungs as we inhale, it then needs to be distributed all the way through our bodies. The exhale, which discharges carbon dioxide externally, also acts as a pump for this internal distribution of oxygen. Yet most of us are only told to inhale deeply, with little or no attention given to the manner in which we exhale. Key breathing is a most effective method for distributing oxygen to all parts of the body, as it teaches us how to inhale and exhale fully and completely.

Before learning the techniques of key breathing, it is important to recognize the divergent rhythms, movements and depths in the ways we breathe. If you watch someone falling asleep you will see how breathing patterns change during the transition from a waking to a sleeping state. You may be aware of this when you fall asleep.

Small babies and animals—unless they are ill—breathe properly, naturally and without thinking about it. When they breathe, their chests and abdomens rise and fall, contracting and expanding on each inhale and exhale. Their torsos flex and release as breath moves through their bodies. You can even observe—though not as distinctly—the breath moving into the limbs. Watch the tiny movements, like subtle throbbings of a current as it passes through the arms, fingers, legs, feet and toes.

Adults, however, need to become aware of their breathing patterns and to consciously choose to modify poor habits in order to breathe properly again.

Most adults breathe too shallowly. Watch yourself breathe and you will probably see very little movement throughout your body's structure. There may be small ripples of motion in your chest or abdomen, and your shoulders may rise a bit as you inhale and fall as you exhale. If your breathing is isolated in the area of your nose, mouth and throat, it may even appear that your breath does not affect your general body activity whatsoever.

Try breathing this way: Inhale taking in oxygen as you normally would. As you exhale try to feel where the breath you have taken into your body is now moving. Most say they do not feel much of anything. When we direct them to exhale more fully, they push the breath out of their mouths harshly, in a shallow puff or gust. This produces the type of exhale one makes when exercising rapidly or running. But as you exhale normally, discharging carbon dioxide, you should feel the breath you released traveling through your entire body— chest, abdomen, groin, arms, legs, extremities—everywhere.

Now try breathing another way. As you inhale for a count of five, let your shoulders and your chest rise up (do not hunch them, let them rise up with the inhale) and let your abdomen move, too. As you exhale for a count of five to ten, utter a big sigh of relief out loud and let the breath go out as long and as far as you can. Keep sighing out loud, letting go of everything. Feel your shoulders loosen, your chest go inward, your back and your pelvis relax. At the completion of the exhale, you may even feel a sensation like a current traveling through your groin and into your legs and feet, as well as through your arms and hands. Does that feel different from the way you feel when you exhale normally? To us it feels better.

Most of us have felt the release in a sigh and a deep exhale as an involuntary reflex to relieve tension. But that usually occurs without our planning it or thinking about it. Now that we are conscious of the feeling, we realize we can call upon it whenever we like. But why does it feel so good? Dr. Elsworth Baker, president of the American College of Orgonomy (and author of *Man in the Trap*), explains:

> When we breathe in and out, we experience a complete pulsation of the body. Breathing in produces the contraction phase while...breathing out produces the expansion phase of the pulsation....Expansion is a pleasurable sensation. Thus, when we breathe out, we feel pleasure. A prolonged exhale, accompanied by a sigh, increases this pleasurable feeling. Additionally, during expansion, more blood reaches the tissues than during contraction. This means that the tissues are being oxygenated to a greater extent during exhalation. Because of this, we experience a greater—an enhanced—sense of being alive.

What Judy and I know, because we have experienced it, is that key breathing feels marvelous! In an era when we are being told by doctors to listen to our own bodies, we believe the most urgent first step is to become aware of our breathing and learn how to use it to enhance our well-being.

For both of us, key breathing does reduce tension and stress. It prevents or curtails feelings of anxiety. A moment or two of key breathing can warm our hands or feet when they are cold. Key breathing can also relieve premenstrual cramps, backaches and oncoming headaches. It enables us to offset sleeplessness, helps us to think more clearly, eliminates confusion from our lives. There are specific instructions for a Key Breathing Exercise in Part III of this book.

Does it sound as if we are hawking some system that uses a magic elixir? We are. The system is called key breathing, and the elixir is human breath.

VISUALIZATION

Visualization, or seeing with the "mind's eye," is the process by which we form a mental picture of something. It is an extremely potent tool that allows imagined things to take on a substance that makes them seem real to us and allows us to experience them throughout our faces and our bodies.

Learning how to visualize and acting out your visualizations when you exercise is the key to getting the maximum benefits from your exercise time, to building and maintaining a positive self-image, and projecting that self-image to others. Developing the habits of key breathing and visualization is at the root of feeling good and feeling good about yourself.

Actors visualize all the time, in life and in work. Imagine going through a dreadful day with a bad cold, a runny nose that resembles Rudolph the Red-Nosed Reindeer, a sore throat and teary eyes; a day when your car breaks down, you lose a job you want, and have problems at home. Then think about how it would be to have to get all "fluffed up" in some glamorous outfit, do a complete makeup and coiffure and bounce into some benefit dinner with a thousand people who expect you to be beautiful, gracious and friendly. Or think of having to go on the set to play a scene in which you are to exude charm, wit, intelligence and physical stamina.

In order to make the transition from feeling ill, discouraged and frumpy to feeling well, enthusiastic and attractive, you need to visualize yourself as a person with good health, good looks and high spirits. When you can visualize in this positive way, it changes the way you look and feel and changes the way you seem to others.

Professionally, we actors are constantly having to create something that does not, in actuality, exist in order to make a production and characterization work. We have to imagine a situation that appears only on the paper of the script, then begin to see pictures of it and of ourselves or our character within the situation. We have to set about visualizing and then projecting the thoughts, feelings, tones of voice, attitudes and movements that will make the situation and character come to life in a performance believable to ourselves and to an audience.

One fundamental example of how visualization is utilized in acting occurs in the earliest days of many acting classes. The teacher might tell the new student to "stand up and be

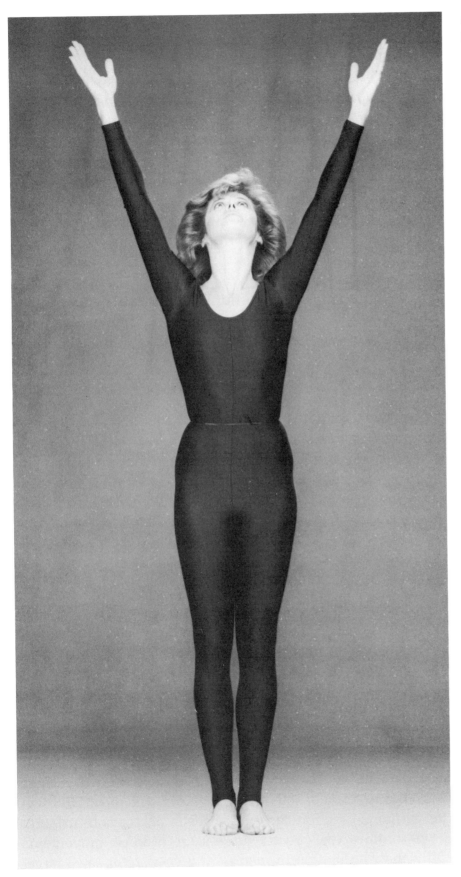

Acting out my visualization of a stately pine tree

a tree." The student might think, "Nuts! What kind of the-atrical claptrap is this? I came here to learn how to act as a human. I'm a person, not a tree!"

When this happened to me years ago, I stood up feeling like a self-conscious blob. But then I decided to let my imagination take over and began to visualize a tree. When I tried acting out what I visualized, it worked!

Try it. Stand up and be a tree. Select one type of tree and visualize it in your mind's eye. Then begin to emulate it with your face and as many parts of the body as you can use.

Are you a weeping willow, all limp and loose? Are you a stately pine, growing skyward from a broad, sturdy trunk, with rigid foliage? Try it both ways. Add some other trees if you like and try those. What you visualize will make a difference in how you think. How you think will determine and direct your feelings. How you feel will make a difference in how you stand. (A pale, slender-trunked tree will not stand the same as a dark, thick-trunked one.) How you stand will make a difference in how you look. Go to the mirror. Don't feel embarrassed; nobody is there but you. Try it first with the willow and then with the tall pine, or with any other type of tree you wish to visualize.

Now expand your visualization to include the weather sur-rounding your tree. See the weather in your mind's eye and direct that picture onto your face and body. Is it still or is there a gentle breeze or a gale-force wind blowing? Visualize it all those ways; then direct each picture into your attitudes and movements.

Study yourself in the mirror. Watch how your face and the different parts of your body move and look with one tree, then another. Observe how the tree pictures you make in your mind change your attitude, your appearance, your feelings about yourself.

Visualization is a crucial element in exercise. What you project when you exercise has a great deal to do with what you project in your daily life. If, during a workout, you jump up and down and flail your arms and legs about mindlessly, your aerobic fitness may increase, but you will not be en-hancing your self-image. Surely you do not want to project yourself in your daily activities as a person who moves through life without direction, unable to focus on the job at hand. Suppose, however, you try these same exercise movements and visualize them performed with precision; or see a target for your hands or feet when they are extended; or capture a feeling in your mind's eye that you project into your body. Then you would be exercising and creating a positive self-image at the same time. The visualizations of Superlife can do that for you. They also help you to know what you should feel as you do each exercise properly, in order to receive its full benefits.

To be specific about the various types of visualization techniques and how they enhance exercise time and daily living as well, let's identify the five methods of visualization we suggest using in Superlife.

1. Visualize something other than yourself in your mind's eye and then "act out" that visualization. It is very like the experiment you just completed with the tree. You will also see this method employed in many of the Superlife exercises in Part III.

2. Visualize your own physical, mental and emotional energies as real substances—blended together into one resource that you can mobilize and direct to various parts of your body. Your energy can be directed by a combination of holding the picture of it in your mind's eye, key breathing and visualizing your energy's movement to whatever destination in your body you select. To start with, you may wish to also utilize an imagined situation.

Try this one now, wherever you are. Extend your right hand as though you were casually saying goodbye to someone. Put out your hand and close it around the imagined hand you are going to shake. Now shake that visualized hand. Next, do the same thing, but first visualize a situation in which the hand you will shake belongs to a person who could be dangerous to someone you love. As you shake the other hand, see and feel your need to restrain that person from leaving. Let your grip and your handshake become energized with your need to forcefully control that person until your loved one is out of harm's way. Hang on, and exhale as you direct your energy down your arm and into your grasp. Work at it!

If I had photographed your handshaking in both of the situations described above, both sets of photos would have looked reasonably alike with regard to the external physical motions. Your right hand probably would have been extended the same distance in each case. It would have been seen making a clasping motion, then moving up and down for the handshake. But when you altered your visualization, you created a very different energy and infused it, first one kind, then the other, into your seemingly identical movements, making them not at all alike internally. When you visualize during Superlife exercises you learn how the exercises should *feel*, thus you work your body much more effectively.

3. Another simple way to visualize during exercise is to picture the exact target at which you are aiming a hand or foot. In other words, you line up the target first, executing the move slowly once or twice to visualize the line between your hand and the target, or between your foot and the target. Then, when you execute the move more rapidly (whether one time or several times in an exercise repetition), you will have a precise, visualized goal for your movement.

As an example, wherever you are now, try a target visualization. Keep your right hand in your lap. Then raise your right arm, and extend it fully in front of you, pointing out with your right index finger as you do. Do this five times in rapid succession, returning your hand to your lap and then thrusting it out, pointing the index finger as described. If you had marked the air where your fingertip touched each time, you would probably have five different marks in the air. Now line up a point on the opposite wall or visualize a button suspended in the air in front of you. Do the same exercise twice, very slowly, to line up your movement with the target point on the far wall or with the button you visualized as your target in midair.

Then do five repetitions ("reps") rapidly, each time aiming at your visualized target. If you marked the air where your extended fingertip touched on this set of reps, you should have the same marks for each of the five reps, or at least five marks a great deal closer together.

This type of visualization is used in the development of hand-eye and foot-eye coordination. And good coordination helps us to move more assuredly—physically and mentally—in life, actively targeting the goals we set for ourselves and our actions in reaching those goals.

4. Dancers use another visualization technique we also recommend, especially for learning *kata* (the dancelike, prearranged exercise forms of Advanced Superlife—see Part IV); this method allows you to memorize a routine by visualizing it. In kata, as in dance, we learn a series of moves that are linked together. Then, in order to memorize that sequence—to make it a natural part of ourselves—we visualize ourselves performing the series of movements. We do this rehearsing in our mind's eye while we shower, wash the dishes and go about our daily tasks.

Once we have the routine down pat—as a result of visualizing and practicing it—we begin to visualize it being executed exquisitely. We may not actually achieve the perfection of technique we visualize, but it sets a high standard of excellence toward which we can aim.

5. The final and more personal method that Judy and I used in Superlife exercises is employed to express a positive or negative feeling.

For example, if one of us has a big challenge to be met later in the day or week, we might be feeling a need to stretch our capabilities to meet it head on and handle it well. During the Superlife stretches, we will actually visualize the challenge and practice stretching toward it. Feeling yourself extending toward a goal, working your whole body toward the visualized goal, gives you a strong sense that you are able to stretch out to achieve your objective.

The same thing holds true when practicing the balances. Perhaps I am being approached by some people who are arguing their point of view on a subject. Simultaneously, another group is espousing the opposite point of view on the same matter. What I need most is to maintain my own center, balance the arguments being presented to me, and make a decision as to what should be done. When I visualize this situation during balance exercises and center my breathing, I reaffirm the sense that I will be able to make balanced and rational decisions when I finish exercising.

If it is my own strength and focus I need to reaffirm, I visualize the life situation for which I need them, then express my feeling of strength and positive action in the punching and kicking reps.

Visualizing also helps us to express negative feelings, either when we are angry or frustrated about a specific problem, with another person or situation, or with our own ability to handle a problem in the best way. The problem might not even be a specific one but merely a frustration with the way things are going or a sense that there is too little time to handle all of our responsibilities. In any case, we visualize either the vague or specific cause of our discontent. Then we can use the punch-and-kick reps to strike out at or push away the source of our distress. If the root of the displeasure is in ourselves, we would rather release that feeling by doing the visualization in the reps than to punish ourselves somehow with stored-up self-hostility. If someone else is at the root of the negative feeling, neither Judy nor I would think of actually punching or kicking that person or anyone unless we were attacked physically; but punching and kicking a visual picture in the air does not hurt anyone. And it does make us feel better.

Key breathing and visualizing, followed by a deep exhalation at the conclusion of the reps, absolutely help us to unload negative feelings as well as the burden placed on us by carrying them around. When we stop exercising and get back into our daily routines, we cope better and behave more rationally without negative feelings stored inside.

One note of caution about this last type of visualization: Do not become an amateur psychiatrist. Your feeling that you want to strike out at something or someone does *not* mean that you should rid your life of that situation or that person. It merely signifies you have a feeling that needs to be released in a way that will hurt no one and will allow you to become more clearheaded in coping with your life and communicating with those who are a part of it.

BOWING RESPECT

Karate exercises, matches and demonstrations all begin and end with a bow. The bow is a sign of respect and recognition. Respect, for the self and for others, is fundamental to karate and its philosophy.

When bowing, the hands are held straight down at the sides, and the back remains straight as it inclines slightly forward. The chin remains up, with the eyes looking forward.

When you exercise with another person, remember that— as in almost every experience you share with anyone else— you must always recognize the other's presence and his or her own individual ability to affect the outcome of the moment, whether positively or negatively. When you exercise alone, a bow for yourself and your own surroundings is a reaffirmation of your own potential to affect all the moments of your life and your own respect for the health of your body, mind and spirit.

Respect is a sense of honor, esteem and courteous consid-

eration. You must feel it for yourself, before you can feel it for others.

You must treat yourself honorably, work on those elements that need improvement, forgive yourself for not achieving every goal immediately and understand that, as an adult, you are responsible for yourself. The more you practice self-respect, the more generous you will be able to be with others, the more secure and less threatened you will be by another's strengths or weaknesses.

A good place to practice this feeling of regard and recognition is within an exercise system like Superlife, which focuses on all aspects of the self. That is why we recommend that you bow to your own resources—body, mind and spirit—whenever you begin and end your exercise. It is the same reason we recommend bowing to another with whom you work in a cooperating exercise, in a self-defense practice or in a sparring session (if you are trained for that).

Respect is learned. It is well worth practicing, with such an easy movement as a bow, to yourself or to another human being. Think about it as you bow; you will find it to be a restorative moment of good faith.

STRETCH AND FLEXIBILITY

We know that flexibility is a deterrent to injury. Relaxed muscles are not as easily traumatized by impact or sudden movement as tensed muscles. A well-stretched person moves with more fluidity and grace than a rigid, inflexible person. We also believe that stretching increases a muscle's efficient strength. PKA champion Bill Wallace has a master's degree in kinesiology (the science of human muscular movements) and for the ten years Judy has known him, he has maintained that his legendary efficient muscle strength is due largely to stretching. Most karate practitioners agree with him. We do too, because we can feel it and see it at work.

But what about the mind and spirit values of stretching and flexibility? What are these besides physical attributes? A lot! The ability to stretch and be flexible in our thoughts and attitudes is required of us every day of our lives. Of course there are a number of daily tasks we encounter so frequently that dealing with them becomes automatic. But there are important moments that challenge us, and those require us to move out beyond what is known and familiar, to function in new territory. That's when we have to stretch and be flexible.

When a new job is in the offing, when we ask for a raise, when we enter a negotiation, we have to stretch and be flexible. When we need to confront someone in a relationship, join closer to someone or separate from him or her, we have to stretch and be flexible. These same attributes are required when a new baby comes, when an older child enters adolescence, if we change our environment or when we try to counsel a troubled friend. So it is important to work an exercise system that not only stretches the body but offers a means to stretch the mind and spirit as well.

Visualizing as you do Superlife exercises is the means by which you accomplish this "three-way stretch." Suppose it is a new job you are after, or a raise. When you picture that goal while performing Superlife stretches, you unify your mind, body and spirit toward its pursuit. When you can "see" what you want and practice reaching out for it effectively, your belief in your own spirit for doing the same thing in life is reaffirmed.

When you practice your Superlife stretches, visualizing a new element of life (a new relationship, new job, new home, new child or even a new aspect of one of these), you see and feel your own inherent ability to be flexible. And physical, mental and spiritual flexibility is necessary for survival.

We can make up all the fabulous rules we want for how our activities and relationships will unfold throughout the course of any day, but how many of those days actually work out the way we expect them to? The car won't start, the train is late or the bus or subway breaks down. It rains when it was supposed to be sunny. The shoes don't work with the dress, the boss or coworker is in a snit or one of the kids calls from school with a temperature. Something will assure that the old adage proves true, the one that says, "Nothing is permanent but change."

It is our flexibility that provides us with our means of adjusting, of coping with the unexpected, of "spinning on a dime" to make a new order out of the chaos created when things do not turn out as planned. It is flexibility that gives us our ability to compromise, another essential life tool.

By visualizing your own life situations when you practice Superlife joint rotations and stretches, you will feel yourself getting into physical, mental and spiritual shape for the demands of everyday life adjustments and changes. If you can do it in one place, you can do it in the others. Life is, as everyone knows, the biggest exercise of them all.

FOCUS: ATTITUDES AND ACTIONS

One of the problems we find with certain types of exercise is that they are without focus. What does that mean? Often one can spend an hour exercising, jumping up and down, huffing and puffing, arms and legs being raised and lowered, first one

way, then another, but frequently focus comes only at the moment when pain (the burn) is experienced.

For most people nothing is wrong with such an unfocused workout; but for us something is missing. Exercising in this manner reminds us of how life occasionally seems—automated, yet chaotic, repetitious, desensitized until something hurts so much that all we can focus on is the pain.

We believe exercising should be focused and specific in order to offer the most positive benefits. It should provide you with defined, clear ideas and images of what you seek, not only in exercise but in other areas of your life as well, and suggest distinct ways to achieve those goals.

Superlife exercises develop just such a strong focus tool. They teach you to visualize a target or goal; and to direct your total energy toward that goal. Focusing your attitudes and actions while you exercise helps develop the habit for approaching life that way also.

Nearly every corporate expert who writes on important factors in business success tells us that a clear, positive focus in attitudes and actions is perhaps the greatest single factor in the making or breaking of a career. We are told that those whose attitudes and actions focus on drive, assertiveness, positive accomplishment, the ability to rebound from failure, perceptiveness about others and high personal expectations are the achievers and will be valued in any enterprise.

Superlife exercises are designed to develop clear, positive focus in attitude and action. Practicing the exercises with the tools provided will help you to function with greater clarity in every aspect of your life.

BALANCE AND CENTERING

There is a distinct advantage to having better-than-average balance skills for all physical activity. Any exercise that requires you to stand on one leg, rise onto your toes, position your body at an unfamiliar angle or shift your weight smoothly from side to side demands good balance skills. Most people can stand, walk and run without falling down, so they presume they have all the balance skills needed in life.

But karate necessitates particularly finely tuned balance. Standing on one leg while kicking with the other is one ob-

vious example. Performing kata (see Advanced Superlife in Part III) requires solid balance for smooth, flowing transitions between the movements. When two people spar in a karate class or practice self-defense, both need well-developed balance. It is one thing to have adequate balance for your own exercises, quite another to maintain that balance when another person counters to every move you make.

In Superlife, balance goes beyond a physical skill to encompass a personal character attribute. So, just as with stretch, flexibility and focus, balance is treasured for the enhancement it brings to your physical, mental and emotional well-being.

Daily decisions require us to balance one side of the coin against the other. When we present ideas, negotiate, conclude sales or conduct personal relationships, we must balance factors such as differences of opinion that may come from diverse age, sex, economic, social or religious backgrounds.

Think of how frequently we use the word "balance" to signify equilibrium in every aspect of life. The extremes of unhealthy eating are called anorexia and bulimia; but a person who eats healthily consumes "a well-balanced diet." People who suffer from enormous highs and lows are, at the extreme, manic depressives. Others, capable of maintaining a stable emotional life, are called "well-balanced." Those who take things in order of importance are able to "balance their priorities." And justice itself, in the law of the land, is visualized as a set of scales, or balances. Balance is the key to harmony and fair play in nearly every aspect of our daily lives.

Good balance helps to keep us from being "pushovers." While each of us may elect to be a pushover in one particular moment, none of us wants to be a compulsive pushover—physically, mentally or emotionally—all the time.

Superlife—by providing an entire series of exercises devoted to balance, and weaving balance throughout its integrated system—helps to develop a strong center from which our attitudes and actions can flow.

Centering, finding and maintaining your own core, is spoken about constantly in every type of Eastern exercise. Expressions such as "I have to find my center," "Keep it centered," or "Move from your center" are used repeatedly among the practitioners. As with the other doctrines, the multiple life values of centering were identified and incorporated into Eastern exercise systems many centuries ago.

The Chinese call the center *tan-tien* ("tahn-tien"), the Japanese version being *tan den* ("tahn den"). Both cultures identify the center as a point in the lower abdomen, approximately two-thirds of the way down between the navel and the pubic bone. They believe that your life energies (*chi* in Chinese, *ki* in Japanese) are collected and stored there, with the center working as your body's natural energy accumulator.

We suggest that when you move, you think of that moment as originating from your center in the lower abdomen. No matter what part of your body you are moving or what move you are making, realize that the center of your energy (in your abdomen) empowers that movement.

Try it as you walk or exercise. Being aware of that abdominal center should give you a stronger sense of balance and stability. As you practice Superlife exercises, awareness of your center will become natural, not requiring intense concentration. Once that has happened, you can work toward investing more power into your movements. When you inhale and exhale with key breathing from that center, your balance skill will improve greatly.

Should you find yourself feeling "thrown" by something in everyday life, you can use this technique to restabilize yourself. Sitting, standing or lying down, take a few key breaths with full exhales from your center. Nobody will know you are doing it, and it will reinforce your perception that you are able to regain balance and cope well with the situation.

RELAXATION AND STRESS MANAGEMENT

Stress is one of the primary causes of athletic injuries, migraine headaches, ulcers, lung ailments, cirrhosis of the liver, cancer, coronary heart disease, depression and suicide. It contributes to the onset of such illnesses as diabetes, genital herpes and multiple sclerosis. Could there be any question that we all need to know how to relax?

Thirty years ago, Thomas Holmes, a psychiatrist affiliated with the University of Washington and working with psychologist Richard Rahe, developed a scale to measure specific stressful events and their impact on the human system. The

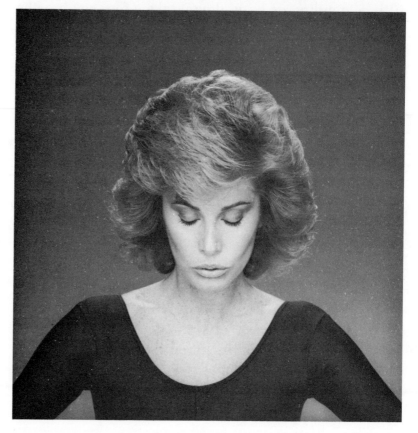

Holmes–Rahe scale has shown that among the most stressful events are such negative experiences as the death of a spouse or a close family member, divorce, marital separation and imprisonment. But the scale has also informed us of the high rates of stress produced by such joyous events as pregnancy, birth, marriage, buying a new home and Christmas.

Why is our concern with stress so much greater today than it was three decades ago? Then, as now, pregnancy, birth, marriage, marital problems, new houses, death and Christmas were all parts of the fabric of life. True, the divorce rate has risen, but the childbirth rate has declined; and people live longer now, thanks to advances in modern science.

Perhaps, as Dorothy Parker said, "It's not the tragedies that kills us...it's the messes." As life has become increasingly more complex, decisions and pressures besiege us during every waking hour. And many of us carry that stress over into our sleep and our dreams. Today, relaxation that requires an escape for a considerable period of time on a regular basis is almost never possible—at least not frequently enough to offset the cumulative damage caused by a chronically stressed existence.

The rare exception to this dilemma occurs during exercise periods...sometimes. Though most exercise produces a release from stress, certain exercises actually cause stress or injury. Exercises that instruct you to bounce to increase stretch, overextend your knee, elbow or neck joints, jump repeatedly on hard surfaces or keep your lower back arched can be the direct cause of bodily harm. The same is true for instructions to exercise when you are already pained from the experience. Exercises that encourage an unhealthy brand of competition, belittling you for not being as conditioned or as expert as someone else, can cause mental and emotional stress.

Productive exercise systems should give you protective physical advice and encourage you to work hard to develop at your own level. They should also present guidelines for how you should feel while exercising and suggest reachable goals. Additionally, they should provide you with specific instructions for exercising in a relaxed state and with a method for maintaining or recapturing that state in the course of your daily activities.

None of us can actually eliminate stress from our lives, nor should we wish to. Some of life's best moments are stressful, as the Holmes–Rahe scale tells us. And healthy competition should be a positive experience. But all of us need to be able to manage stress to be in control of the harmful effects it can produce and to counter its negative impact with an ever-ready relaxation mechanism.

Here's how stress works. The body's energy system consists of a three-part cycle: tension, charge and release. The tension phase feels like a gathering of electrified energy. As with electrical energy, the body's charge phase occurs when that gathered energy has reached its tolerable capacity. With electrical energy, the charge sets off an automatic release, but this is not so in many human bodies. People are taught to hold things in, so when the charge does not activate a release, the body's energy cycle gets stuck in first gear and tension persists, continuing to build. That gathered, unprocessed overload of tension is what we call stress. And it is enormously debilitating.

Several recent developments provide a means of counteracting stress. The key breathing and visualization techniques employed throughout Superlife utilize many of the same principles found in meditation and biofeedback. When you exercise and key-breathe in the morning, you set up a pattern and rhythm for relaxed breathing throughout the day. You are reminded that you own a wonderful weapon—your own breath—that can melt away the cumulative burden of stress, and that you can use the weapon anywhere, at any time. In any situation where tension mounts to make you feel "uptight," use a few key breaths to unblock your energy cycle and move it along to the charge and release phases.

Judy and I learned key breathing some years ago from the late Dr. Albert I. Duvall, Fellow in the American College of Orgonomy. Until recently, other physicians with whom we had discussed it had often seemed skeptical. Now all that is changing.

Time magazine's June 6, 1983, issue had a cover headline called "Seeking Cures for Modern Anxieties." The feature article was entitled "Stress: Can We Cope?" and the subhead read: "As modern pressures take their toll, doctors preach relaxation." The story told of a program at Boston's Beth Israel Hospital that "uses techniques of easing stress to fight hypertension." Time went on to explain the hospital's "relaxation techniques (watching your breath go in and out)," of "keeping your thoughts focused" and of the value of finding "a quiet center." Sound familiar?

Judy and I cannot administer tests and evaluations that are part of the hospital's program. But we can provide you with the gift of Superlife exercises, its key breathing and its techniques for visualization and centering, which are very like the basics of many formalized stress-management programs. This gift has given each of us the ability to remain comfortable in our own skin.

PART III

SUPERLIFE EXERCISES

MAXIMIZING EXERCISE BENEFITS

Superlife exercises are designed to shape, tone and firm every part of your body. For shaping your body, the most valuable tool is exercising so that all the muscles involved are being fully worked. That's far more important than how fast you exercise, the height of your leg extensions or any other factor.

Using the visualization and breathing accompanying each exercise will help you to know how you should feel when doing the exercises properly. From the photos, you can see that, having exercised a lot, I am extremely flexible. Perhaps you are, too. If not, start with much shallower bends and lower kicks, using generally less radical body positions. But be sure you can actually feel your muscles working. As you improve your conditioning, your flexibility will increase.

Though you probably know that everyone should consult a physician before embarking on an exercise program of any sort, please remember this is especially important if you suffer from any current or chronic illness, either physical or mental, which might be adversely affected by exercise.

HOW TO VISUALIZE

Hold a picture in your mind's eye and direct it into other parts of your body.

Then, assuming whatever starting position is given for the exercise you are about to do, visualize in one or more of the following ways, as elaborated on pages 49 to 51.

Acting out my visualization of a
weeping willow tree

1. As actors do, see yourself as something or someone other than yourself and then act out the visualization. Specific suggestions are offered with the Superlife Exercises that follow.

2. Use only the image of your own physical, mental and emotional energies and envision how you would mobilize and direct them. See and feel them move through your body.

3. Focus visualization on an imagined target, either in mid-air, where a person or object might be, or select a mark on the wall or on another existing object, and move to aim for that target.

4. As dancers do, picture a technique or series of movements in your mind's eye as it would be executed in its most perfect form, so you can approach duplicating that performance.

5. Visualize something or someone in your life—either specific or general—that makes you want to express a positive or negative feeling, and use your movement to express that.

ABOUT KEY BREATHING

As you learn to do key breathing, many new sensations will occur in your body. Because they are unfamiliar, some may give you a temporary sense of anxiety. If you understand some of the following about what occurs when you key-breathe, you will not feel apprehensive.

1. What key breathing does—It produces a more complete body pulsation than other types of breathing. The combination of contraction on the inhale and expansion on the exhale comprises the pulsation. Key breathing makes the expansion phase of the breath deeper, more complete and more relaxing. It produces sensations of aliveness that may, at first, seem strange but will later become pleasurably familiar.

2. How key breathing works on you—As you inhale and exhale in a prolonged, full manner, you allow more oxygen and, thus, more energy to circulate to more parts of your body. As you key-breathe, you may feel a looseness in your body that is unfamiliar, or perhaps you'll feel a tingling sensation. These new sensations may make you anxious, causing you to wonder if something bad is happening. In fact what produces the looseness or tingling is merely energy reaching previously unfed parts of your body, relaxing and nourishing you more completely. This same feeling that, at the start, may make you apprehensive will later become the source of great waves of pleasure and relaxation for you.

3. Other sensations felt in key breathing—"Looseness" and "tingling" have already been described. "In contact" and "out of contact" are also handy key breathing expressions. To be in contact is to be relaxed and in touch only with physical sensations of your own body and its breathing process. To be out of contact is to have your mind wander elsewhere, to be in other than the reality of that moment where there is only you and your breathing. Try to remain in contact as you practice. Stop if you go out of contact.

"Letting go" is the final instant of the exhale when air is released in a total surrender to relaxation.

4. Who should not practice prolonged key breathing?—The American College of Orgonomy cautions that:

· If you have a history of heart problems, consult your physician before doing a session of concentrated key breathing.

· If you are epileptic, you should not do a deep session, but less concentrated key breathing can be performed from time to time.

· Anyone with a known history of psychosis should refrain from prolonged breathing sessions.

As your breathing becomes deeper and more centered, and as exhalation moves through your solar plexus, you will feel a calming effect. The solar plexus, located in the center of the diaphragm, contains the ganglia (or networks of nerves), which send nerve impulses into the abdomen and to all vital organs: heart, lungs, liver, kidneys, intestines and stomach. As circulation in the solar plexus increases with key breathing practice, you will feel a rejuvenating, calming effect on your entire nervous system.

Benefits: Key breathing relaxes facial muscles and eyes; reduces physical, mental and emotional stress; oxygenates the entire body and improves balance, centering and focus.

Visualization: Visualize your breath as an active, tangible part of you, one that transports oxygen, energy and relaxation to every other part of your body. See your breath as a real substance, one whose motion you can easily direct.

Breathing: Inhale through your nose, mouth closed. Exhale with mouth open and, when possible, make an audible noise—a sign, a groan—whatever comes out naturally.

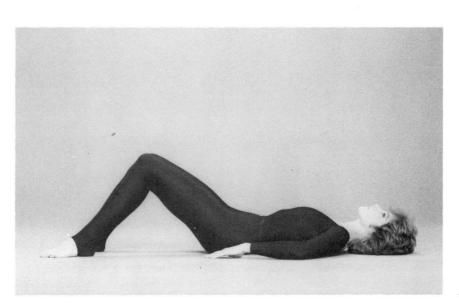

1. Lie down on your back, on a bed or on an exercise mat. Your arms are at sides, your elbows slightly curved, your palms down. Bend your knees, place your feet flat on the floor a few inches apart and allow your knees to fall apart in a relaxed way, without pulling your upper thigh muscles inward. Keep your chin up.

2. Keep your arms at your sides as in step 1 (my own arms are outstretched in the photos from now on so you can see the body position while breathing). Inhale deeply—but not sharply—through your nose, allowing your shoulders, chest and abdomen to rise with your breath.

(continued on next page)

3. Begin to exhale through your open mouth, making noise out loud. Let your shoulders, chest and abdomen drop while you exhale.

4. Continue to exhale, visualizing your breath moving through your solar plexus, abdomen, pelvis, thighs, legs and feet and, as your shoulders and chest drop further, into your arms, hands and fingers. Keep making audible noise. Release your last bit of breath tilting your pelvis upward, allowing your head to fall back with your chin tilted up a bit. (This is the position of the completely relaxed "letting go" phase of key breathing.

Reps: Inhale and exhale in this manner for no longer than 2 minutes to start, prolonging the session as you grow comfortable with it.

Incorrect position—back is arched.

NOTE:

· If you start to lose contact or feel your eyes wander, stop for a moment, relax and try again.

· If you feel an electriclike current in your hands or lips, stop until that sensation passes, then resume key breathing.

· If you feel frightened by the movement of energy, stop for a moment. Remind yourself that it is merely energy moving to unfamiliar parts of your body, regenerating you in a relaxed, healthy manner. Once you feel safe, resume breathing practice.

· You can do one or more key breaths either sitting or standing. Just breathe properly (keeping your audible noise to just a sigh if you are in public), and allow your body to move subtly in the same way it does when you key-breathe lying down: shoulders and chest dropping, back released with pelvis tipped upward, head dropped slightly back.

MAKING A FIST

Making a fist is very simple. You need only do the following:

1. Open your hand with your fingers raised and together, your thumb out from your palm.

2. Close your fingers down until they touch your palm.

3. Curl your fingers under as far as you can, and close your thumb over outside of your curled fingers.

Reps: To practice, make a fist 5 times with your left hand, 5 times with your right, then 5 times with both hands simultaneously.

NOTE:
· Remember that when you strike with a fist, you will want to connect with flat surface between your large and middle knuckles. Always strike with your wrist straight and hand positioned so that this will be the "hitting" surface.
· Always *snap* back your arm after punching out with your hand in the fist position. This will prevent elbow strain. Think of how a towel snaps back at you the instant after it makes its full extension.

MAKING A PALM-HEEL THRUST

Any technique with the words "palm heel" in its name means that you will strike with the heel of the palm of your hand. In order to make a palm heel, do the following:

Thrust your hand out in front of you so that the heel, or fleshy, lower portion, of the palm leads out and connects with the target. Keep the upper part of your hand—with all your fingers together and thumb in close—bent backward. (If you actually strike something or someone, this protects your fingers by allowing only fleshy portion of palm to absorb the force.)

Reps: Do 5 palm-heel strikes with your left hand, then 5 with your right hand.

NOTE:
· Strong, well-stretched palm-heel reps can be done anywhere and are effective for toning both the lower arm as well as that part of the upper arm that has a tendency to sag.
· You may extend your arm fully on palm-heel thrusts, not snapping the arm back as in punches. The palm-heel hand position takes the strain off of a fully extended elbow.

FRONT KICK

With a front kick, the ball of the foot connects with the target. Practice this foot position as follows:

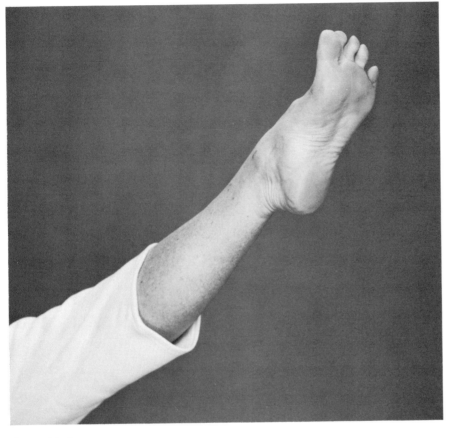

Front Kick

Reps: Kick out with your left foot in a front-kick position 5 times. Then kick out 5 times with your right foot, always remembering to pull your toes back and up so only the ball strikes.

NOTE: Really reach out with the ball of your foot in order to work your calves. To familiarize yourself with foot positions for kicks, you can practice them at any time of the day—sitting on a chair if you like—just so they become habitual. This type of practice will also tone leg muscles.

(continued on next page)

FOOT POSITIONS FOR KICKS

Thrust your left foot forward, with only the ball of the foot leading out to connect with the target. Keep your heel pulled down and back toward back of leg, making sure that your toes are pulled tightly up and back. (This would protect your toes if you were actually kicking at a person or thing.)

BACK KICK

With a back kick, connect only with heel of foot. Practice as follows:

Back kick

Kick your left foot out behind you (hold onto something for balance), leading with your heel. Your toes are pulled back and up for their protection.

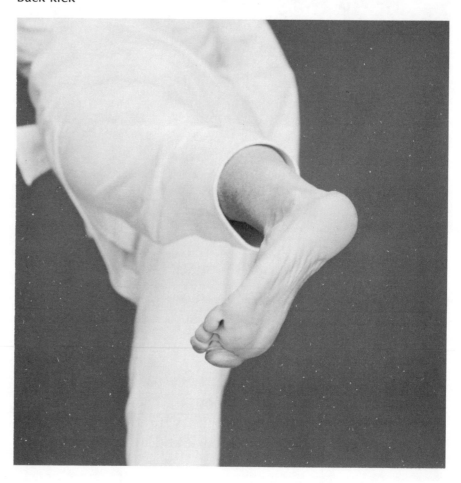

Reps: Kick out to the back with your left foot 5 times, then kick 5 times with your right foot.

NOTE: Keep your kicks low, but reach out with your heel to feel the pull on all the muscles on back of your leg.

SIDE KICK

With a side kick, the outer ridge bone of the foot (from the small toe on down) is what connects with the target. Practice as follows:

Side kick

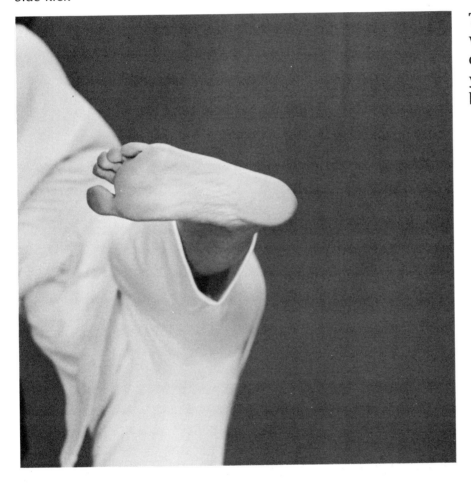

Thrust out your left foot toward your left side, pushing out with outer-ridge bone of your foot. Your toes are pulled back and up for protection.

Reps: Practice 5 times with your left foot, 5 times with your right.

NOTE: On this and other foot position practices, aim very low—slightly off the floor if you wish—in order to concentrate only on the position of foot. Reach out with the ridge bone on the side kick to work your leg muscles.

THE BOW

Benefits: Bowing provides a gentle stretch for the neck and lower back muscles.

Visualization: If you are exercising alone, visualize your own respect for the health of your mind/body/spirit. If you are exercising with another, visualize not only your contribution to the effort but the respect you feel for your partner as well.

Breathing: Inhale as you assume the upright, starting position. Exhale as you bow.

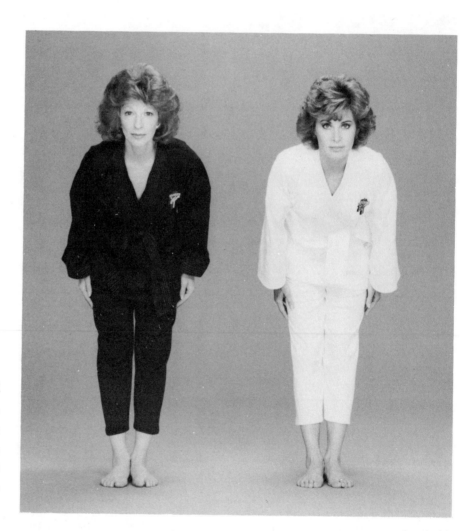

Stand straight with your feet together, hands at your sides. Then, keeping your head up, eyes forward and back straight, bend forward slightly. Resume starting position before breaking the bow.

Reps: Bow 5 times, slowly.

NOTE: This is not a military bow, so stay relaxed. Do not throw your chest out in front or arch your back. Keep your buttocks relaxed and tipped slightly forward.

SCHEDULE FOR SUPERLIFE EXERCISES

EVERY DAY		THREE TIMES EACH WEEK	
Superlife Wake-up:	3 minutes	PKA Power Techniques:	10 minutes
Joint Rotations:	5 minutes	Cooperating Exercises	
Stretches:	7 minutes	(if available):	15 minutes
Balances:	7 minutes		
Superlife Sleep:	3 minutes		
TOTAL	25 minutes		

A daily minimum schedule of 25 minutes will keep you limber, stretched, centered and balanced. Three times a week increase your schedule by adding PKA Power Techniques and Cooperating Exercises. This will give you a more aerobic workout with increased hand–eye and foot–eye coordination, will help with weight reduction and will add more complex stretching for maximum agility and muscle strength.

If no partner is available for Cooperating Exercises, try increasing the reps for all PKA Power Techniques, gradually doubling them so that you are spending approximately 20 minutes on techniques, rather than the 10 minutes needed for the reps originally given. The Cooperating Exercises also act as a cool-down after the techniques. If you eliminate them and substitute additional technique reps, repeat the Joint Rotations at the conclusion as a cool-down.

SUPERLIFE WAKE-UP

These wake-up exercises are to be done very slowly in your bed as you awaken (or on the floor if they would disturb another person who is still asleep in your bed). During sleep, you have been wrapped in a cocoon of slumber, protected from the outside world. In making the transition to the waking state and the activities of your day, you are best prepared if you awaken in slow motion, luxuriously, still feeling the aura of comfort that surrounded your nighttime sleep. Each of the exercises here should be done with long, slow, languid body movements so you can "gentle" yourself into the day.

THE CALENDAR GIRL

(Four-Way Stretch)

Benefits: This unlocks the upper back, shoulders, middle back, lower back, hips and legs—all of which tend to become rigid during the inactivity of sleep.

Visualization: Visualize the beauty of form that is your own body, and see how it moves languidly into exquisite positions as you direct it. Imagining the lovely, elongated stretch associated with the traditional World War II pinup, or calendar girl, enhances your ability to feel the beauty of your body when it moves. (If the notion of a calendar girl seems offensive, try to separate the issues. This is not a pose for the exploitation of your body; it is merely a familiar reference to acknowledge the magnificence of your own human form and the miracle of its beauty in slow motion.)

Breathing: Inhale through your nose as you lie still; exhale each time you stretch for an expansion.

1

2

4

1. Lie flat on your back on the bed, with your feet together, legs straight out, arms outstretched at your sides.

2. Keep your arms outstretched as you roll to left, crossing your bent right knee over your left hip. Exhale as you pull down with your left foot, and touch the bed with your bent right knee. Do not roll over on your side; instead, keep the rest of your body straight to feel the expansion in the middle of your back. Inhale while holding that position.

3. Exhale again, slowly, as you bring your right arm up over your head. Stretch your whole body upward and downward at same time. Feel the elegant elasticity in your body pulling to both sides as well as up and down, simultaneously.

4. Return to the starting position to inhale. Then repeat entire exercise to the right side, crossing your bent left leg, then raising your left arm for a four-way stretch.

Reps: Do this 1 time slowly on each side.

NOTE: Yawn if you like as you exhale and expand in any or all directions. Move slowly and gracefully to ease yourself from sleep.

THE WAKING CAT

Benefits: This gently loosens the back and neck muscles for a smooth transition to daily activities.

Visualization: You are a cat waking from sleep. Each movement is languorous, lazy, long and lean. As a cat, you are in no hurry and want only to feel the luxury of each muscle working slowly before you set out for the day's activities. See your own catlike body as sinewy, moving as though seen through a slow-motion camera.

Breathing: Inhale as you tuck under; exhale slowly and deeply as you arch or stretch, and make a purring sigh if you won't wake anyone in the bed with you.

1. (a) Get on your knees and sit back on heels, curling forward so your head touches the bed with your arms and hands outstretched; (b) lift the fingers of your left hand, stretching your left arm out firmly; (c) lift the fingers of right hand, stretching your right arm out firmly. Lower your hands.

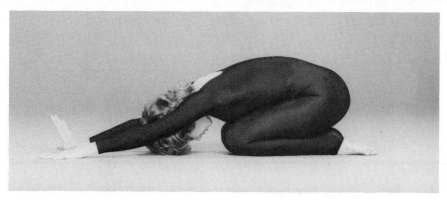

2. Push up with your hands and lift your body off bed, tucking your head and buttocks under, as though chin could reach your pubic bone. Let your back round itself completely.

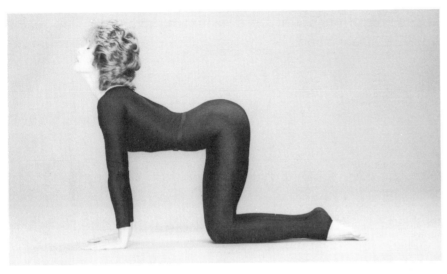

3. Raise head and chin as you raise your buttocks, as though your head and buttocks could touch behind you. Keep your buttocks relaxed and let your back arch completely. Repeat steps 2 and 3 slowly for twenty reps (see instructions below).

4. Keeping your hands in the same position, lower your hips, resting your thighs on the bed, as you straighten your legs, point your toes, and lift your head and chin up and back. Every cat makes this elongated movement before setting out after sleep.

Reps: Do a total of 20 slowly alternating tucks and arches of the waking cat; each separate movement counts as one. Hold the last elongated, stretched arch for 10 seconds.

NOTE:
· Your body is precious. Take the time to feel each movement through every part of it, just as a cat does.
· *Caution:* If you have lower back problems, delete step four.

TOUCH THE SUN AND REACH FOR THE MOON

Benefits: Expands shoulder and neck mobility for the day, and loosens lower back and hips.

Visualization: Aim high to touch the morning's source of all light, heat and energy, so you can continue to reach for it and the moon throughout your waking hours. The sun is high and behind each shoulder.

Breathing: Inhale slowly and deeply when your hands and knees are all on Earth. Do a prolonged exhale as you reach up with either hand.

1. On the bed, get on your hands and knees. Your back is straight, with your head up and eyes forward.

2. Follow your left arm with your eyes as you raise it up and back as high and far behind your left shoulder as possible.

3. Return to starting position and follow your right arm with your eyes as you raise it up and behind your right shoulder to touch the sun and reach for whatever else you desire.

Reps: Alternating your left and right arms, count to 20, reaching for the sun and the moon 10 times with each arm.

NOTE: Move slowly and exhale as you reach for your goals so you give all of yourself to what you aim for.

THE FLOWER

Benefits: This yawn and stretch opens up the chest cavity and diaphragm.

Visualization: See your morning self as a flower that must open slowly to be nourished by all the light it can take in throughout the day. Your arms are petals in slow motion. Your body is your root to the earth.

Breathing: Inhale slowly and fully until your arms are above your head. Exhale, long and deeply, as you open the petals and allow them to separate.

1. Sit on the bed, with your head down and your legs folded in front of you, your hands resting on one another in your lap.

2. Keeping your head down, with your wrists crossed and your hands loose, raise your bent arms until your hands are in front of face.

3. Keeping your wrists crossed, raise your head and arms until your head is straight and your arms are high over your head.

4. Let your head fall back as your arms separate above your head.

5. Lower your arms slowly, opening them totally to the light of day. Return to the starting position.

Reps: Do 1 complete movement to a slow count of 30. Hold 5 long beats at the start, then 5 with your hands over your face, 5 with your arms above your head, 5 as your arms separate, 5 as your arms lower, and 5 back at starting position.

NOTE: Really push the petals open so you can feel the energy in your arms. The more you invest into the movement, the more you will get from it. It also helps to yawn broadly as you open up.

JOINT ROTATIONS

Joints, those spots in the body where two bones join together in a way that allows each of them to move, provide the key to many elements of good health and accident prevention.

They work much like joints in any structure. When properly lubricated, everything runs smoothly. When devoid of lubrication, trouble sets in. Each bodily joint is lubricated by a clear, albuminous fluid called synovia, which is secreted by the membranes of joint cavities and tendon sheaths.

The basics of all flexibility depend on a sufficient supply of synovial fluid. It protects us from many injuries—not only in exercise but also from the too common occurrence of "throwing something out" when we move a certain way in regular, daily motion.

Rotating the joints at the start of each day acts as a motor for production and distribution of synovial fluid. It keeps us from feeling stiff and tight as we move or remain still for long periods. It helps to prevent feeling "locked" in any part of our bodies. It also helps to keep joints oiled so they do not become repositories for uric acid or other substances that can coagulate there to produce arthritis or arthritic sensations.

For this reason, a series of joint rotation exercises—done immediately after getting out of bed—is the best way to ensure feeling well for the entire waking day. These rotations serve as warm-ups in Superlife. They are also recommended as cool-downs or for spontaneous midday exercises to "get out the kinks."

Remember, start any progressive set of exercises from the top of the body and work down. The more flexible and relaxed your head and neck are, the better the rest of your body will respond to exercise or movement of any sort.

Benefits: This loosens neck and shoulder muscles and releases the compression of vertebrae to increase circulation to the brain.

Visualization: Visualize stirring the air around you with your head and neck.

Breathing: Inhale slowly when your head is forward, exhale deeply as your head moves to the sides and backward.

HEAD AND NECK STIR

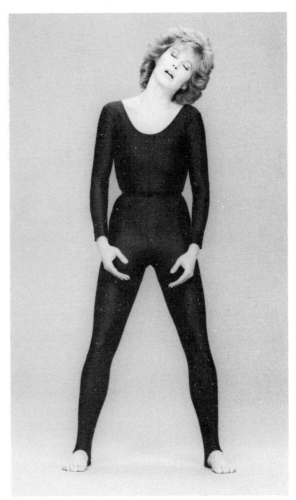

1. Start in a modified horse stance. You should have your feet shoulder-width apart, your knees slightly bent, your arms at sides, your hands in front of thighs, your palms toward center. Your head should be forward so you face the floor, and your buttocks tucked under.

2. Keep your body relaxed and still as you rotate your head and neck slowly to the left, starting your exhale.

(continued on next page)

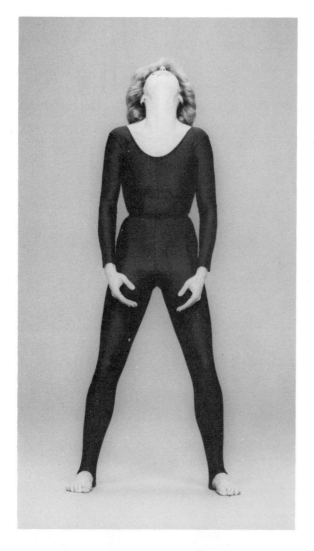 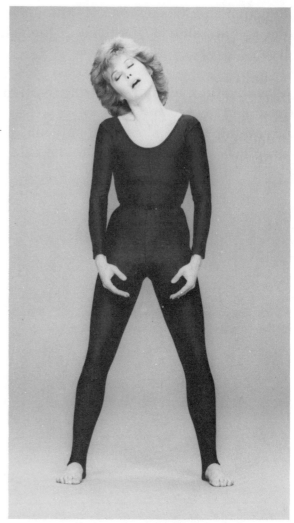

3. Rotate your head and neck backward with your neck relaxed, your mouth falling open for the exhale.

4. Slowly rotate your head and neck to your right shoulder. Then inhale as you rotate your head forward to begin again.

Reps: Do 5 complete slow rotations starting to the left, then 5 to the right. Hold each position for 5 beats.

NOTE:
· To avoid straining delicate neck muscles, backward head motion should not be exaggerated.
· To stay relaxed, keep your pelvis tilted forward and your knees bent.
· On the side positions, feel your ear pulling down to touch your shoulder.

Benefits: This maximizes shoulder mobility to prevent pinched nerves. It also expands chest muscles.

Visualization: While you work your shoulders, see yourself in a pool doing the butterfly stroke, pushing through the water with your arms straight.

Breathing: Inhale and exhale slowly and rhythmically as you butterfly.

BUTTERFLY STROKE

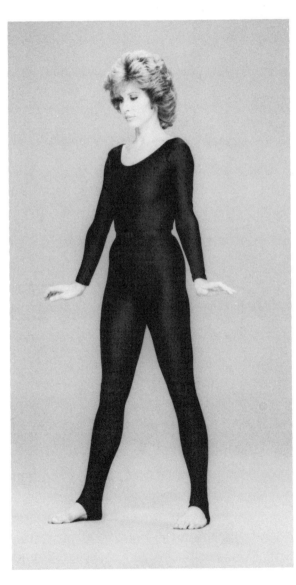

1. Stand with your feet shoulder-width apart, your arms at sides, hands out with palms facing the floor.

2. Raise your arms in front, keeping them straight, and your fingers pulled up and back.

3. Lift your arms up and straight overhead.

4. Rotate your shoulders so your arms are behind you as they come down, and return to the starting position, making a circle.

Reps: Total of 30: Do 5 small-circle rotations as described (like the backstroke), then 5 raising the arms backward at first so you can stroke forward. Repeat the entire exercise, making medium-sized circles. Then repeat again, making large, high circles. (The photographs show me making large circles only.)

NOTE: Push the water on all rotations to utilize the dynamics of tension for firming arm muscles through the entire arm.

Benefits: This improves circulation and elbow mobility and is valuable for preventing or dissolving calcium deposits in the arm joints.

Visualization: Visualize your arms working together with the precision of automobile windshield wipers. (Sometimes we call this "train signals" or "metronome elbows" because each of those images works too.)

Breathing: Inhale and exhale regularly from the abdomen. Breathe in on the strong-man pose, exhale as you extend your arms with your palms upward.

WINDSHIELD WIPERS

1. Start in a horse stance, with your feet almost twice shoulder-width apart, toes pointed out. Bend your knees halfway so you "sit" on the air. Bend both elbows and raise your arms to shoulder height so your fists touch in front of your neck.

(continued on next page)

2. Bring your fists up and out in a strong-man pose.

3. Open your hands palms up and extend your arms straight out.

4. Return to the strong-man pose (step 2).

5. Keeping your elbows straight, drop down your fists and lower arms, facing your knuckles toward the floor.

6. Maintaining straight elbows, push your lower arms up and out straight to the sides, turning your hands so your palms face upward.

Reps: Using both arms together, repeat the complete exercise 10 times.

NOTE:
· Once you are familiar with the moves, do the exercise as a complete rotation at medium speed.
· In a true horse stance, the toes and feet are straight forward, not turned out. If you want to work your inner thighs, feel your thighs pull inward to keep you astride of your "horse." Always keep your buttocks tucked under.

WRIST PROPELLERS

Benefits: Your wrists and hands become flexible.

Visualization: Visualize your wrists as propellors circling in their rotations. Be sure they move cleanly and crisply.

Breathing: Inhale and exhale from the abdomen throughout the exercise.

1. Sitting or standing, hold your right elbow with your left hand; bend your right elbow so your hand is straight up, palm toward center.

2. Keeping your right elbow supported, rotate your right wrist to the left for 5 complete propeller turns.

3. In the same position, rotate your right wrist to the right for 5 complete propellers.

1

2

3

Reps: Do 20 propellers. Make 5 complete circles to one side, then 5 to the opposite side with one hand. Then change hands and again do 5 in each direction.

Benefits: This flexes and strengthens the fingers, knuckles and lower arm muscles.

Visualization: See the air in front of you, and really grab for it. Or visualize something you want and are reluctant to pursue, and really grab for that.

Breathing: Breathe normally from the abdomen, inhaling and exhaling regularly.

CATCHING THE AIR

1. Stand or sit with your elbows bent, hands raised and fingers stretched wide open.

2. Close your hands tightly, as though you have caught what you wanted.

Reps: Using both hands together, count to 20, alternating opening and closing them, for 10 complete open/close reps.

PLAYING THE PIANO

Benefits: This lubricates and loosens the finger and knuckle joints to make hand movements more agile and graceful. People spend much time and money caring for hands and nails. But the essence of beautiful hands lies in the ability to move them with a smooth dexterity.

Visualization: Visualize that you are practicing the piano, and because it has very stiff keys, you must play each key forcefully in order to be heard.
Breathing: Inhale and exhale regularly from the abdomen.

1. Start, sitting or standing, by bending your elbows with palms downward as though to play a keyboard in front of you. Then strike the notes with both pinkies only, keeping your other fingers raised.

2. Leaving your pinkies down, strike the next notes with both ring fingers.

3. Next, hit the notes with the middle fingers of both hands.

4. Now strike the notes with your index fingers.

5. Last, play the notes firmly with both thumbs.

Reps: Play the scale 10 times—5 slowly, then 5 rapidly.

PUNCHING WAIST TWISTS

Benefits: This increases circulation and strengthens and firms waist and back muscles. It also firms inner thigh muscles.

Visualization: Visualize punching a target on either side of you that is slightly taller than you are. You can only reach that target by moving your upper body from the waist and punching out at it.

Breathing: Breathe rapidly for this faster exercise. Exhale and make a noise ("hah") on each punch.

1. Start in a modified horse stance, your feet at shoulder width, pointing straight ahead. Your buttocks are tucked under, with the insides of your thighs gripping inward. Your elbows are bent and in at sides; your hands are in fists with palms up.

2. Do not move your hips as you swivel your upper body to the left and move your right hand across, turning your fist so the palm side is down.

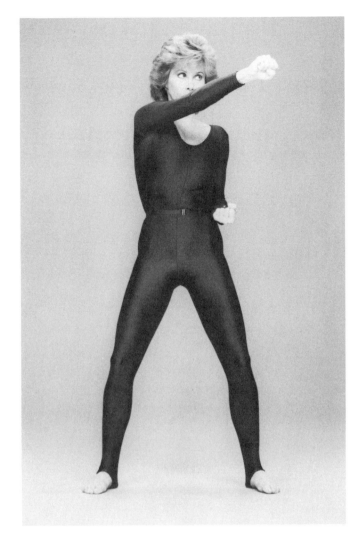

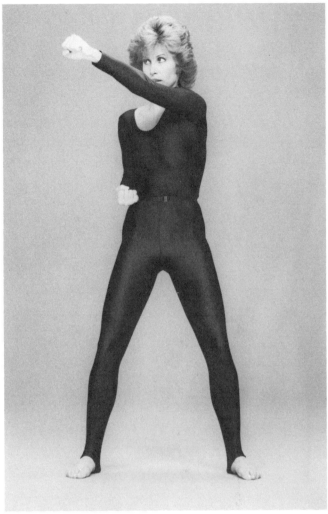

3. Punch hard at the target site with your right fist, *snapping* your arm back quickly to avoid overextending your elbow.

4. Swivel from the waist up only to the right, and punch with the left fist.

Reps: Do 20 punching waist twists in all, alternating quickly each time from one side to the other.

NOTE:
· Be sure to *snap* your punching arm back immediately after the punch so you will not overextend and injure your elbow (think of a towel you snap back quickly).
· Twist only from the waist; keep your buttocks tucked under, and grip the imagined horse you sit on with the insides of your thighs to tighten your inner thigh muscles.

UPPER BODY DIRECTIONALS

Benefits: This releases lower spinal pressure and flexes both the lower-back and abdominal muscles. It also tightens the inner thighs.

Visualization: You are pointing out directions, using only your upper body and head to indicate them. Nothing below your waist should move.

Breathing: Inhale while your head rotates down and forward. Exhale as your head rotates backward.

1. Start in a modified horse stance, your feet separated to shoulder width, pointing forward, your knees slightly bent, buttocks tucked under. Your elbows should be bent, hands on hips.

2. Point to the left with your head and upper body. Stretch your head out as though it is a pointer.

3. Rotate your upper body forward, reaching out with your head; but don't allow your chin to drop to your chest.

4. Point to the right with your upper body and head.

5. Point the way behind you by rotating your head and upper body backward.

Reps: Do 10 full rotations: 5 to left, then 5 to the right.

NOTE:
· Keep your chin straight when your head is forward and when it is lying back to avoid neck strain.
· As with all regular or modified horse stances, if you pull inward with all the muscles of the inner leg (as though gripping a horse), you will be working them toward extraordinary firmness. (Charles Atlas used to call this principle "dynamic tension," and he was right—it works!)

HIP GRINDS

Benefits: This lubricates the hip joints and loosens the spine.

Visualization: The best images are old burlesque routines, because the hip rotations here are similar to burlesque "bumps and grinds."

Breathing: Do normal breathing and exhaling from the abdomen.

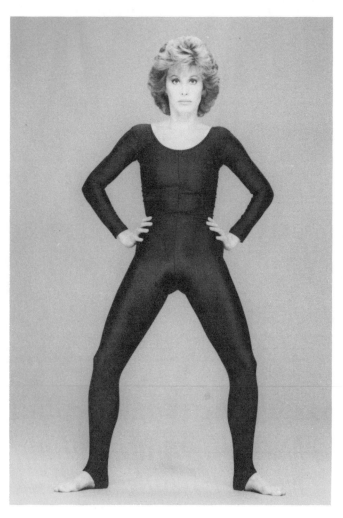 

1. Start in modified horse stance, feet shoulder-width apart, pointed out, knees slightly bent, elbows bent, hands on hips. Begin the grind by tilting your lower pelvis forward, tucking your buttocks under, and leading with the pubic bone.

2. Grind entire lower pelvis to left, leading out with left hip.

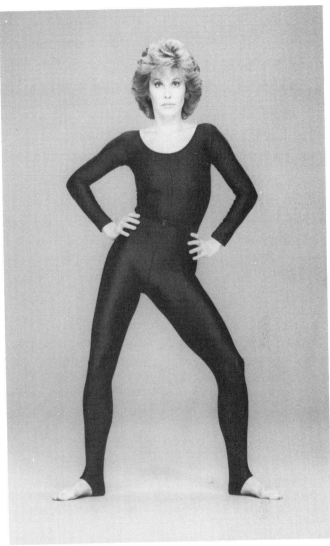

3. Grind the rotation backward, leading with the buttocks and with the back arched.

4. Rotate to right with the lower pelvis, extending the right hip all the way out.

Reps: Start all grinds with forward motion. Do 5 complete rotations to the left, then 5 complete rotations to the right.

NOTE: This exercise gives great hip flexibility, but you really must exaggerate the moves. Remember the old Duke Ellington song: "It don't mean a thing if it ain't got that swing!"

KNEE GRINDS

Benefits: This loosens knees and ankles to help prevent injury. It also strengthens the muscles that support the knees.

Visualization: Visualize stirring the inside of a bowl with your knees.

Breathing: Inhale and exhale from the abdomen normally.

1. To begin, place your feet and legs together with your knees slightly bent and your palms pressed against sides of your knees. Extend your bent knee-caps forward.

2. Rotate both knees to the left, pushing both palms against them.

3. Grind your knees backward, straightening them a bit as you reach back with the backs of your knees.

4. Rotate your knees to the right, pushing your palms against them.

Reps: Do a total of 10 knee grinds, 5 leading to the left side, then 5 to right.

NOTE: Be sure to keep your legs and feet together as you grind, letting your knees do the work rather than your hips.

ANKLE STIRS

Benefits: This loosens the Achilles tendon and shin area, improves arches and prevents sprained or strained ankles by lubricating ankle joints.

Visualization: Your feet are in a bowl filled with a substance that needs stirring. As you stir with your feet, be sure to make full, reaching circles so you wipe the sides of the bowl.
Breathing: Inhale and exhale from the abdomen.

1. Start the exercise either sitting or standing. If standing, hold onto something for support. Lift your right foot a few inches off floor with your toes straight forward.

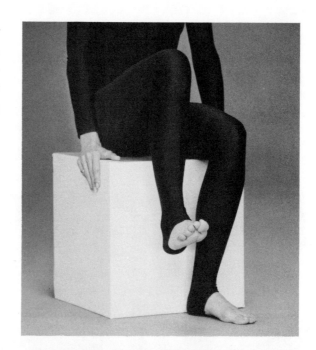

2. Keeping your toes up, twist your ankle to the left.

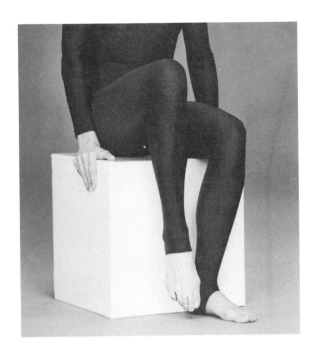

3. Rotate your toes downward and back to feel the pull on the front of the foot.

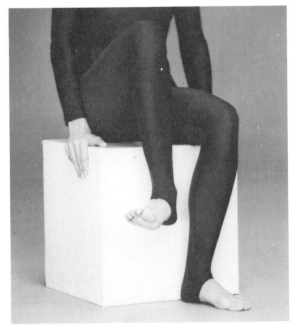

4. Move your toes up as you twist your ankle to the right.

Reps: Do 5 stirs in each direction with the right foot, then 5 more in each direction with the left foot.

NOTE: After you have worked on balance exercises for a while, do ankle stirs while standing, but do not hold on for support.

TOE CATCHES

Benefits: This strengthens arches and prevents rigidity in the toe joints. It also helps prevent foot and toe cramps.

Visualization: Visualize catching the air with your toes.
Breathing: Breathe deeply from the abdomen.

1. Sitting or standing, lift your right foot off the ground with your toes bent up and back to open the "catching" area.

2. Grip your toes tightly shut, as though to grab and hold the air you caught. Repeat with your left foot.

Reps: Do 10 toe catches, 5 with your right foot, then 5 with your left.

NOTE: Toe catches and ankle stirs are extremely useful for relieving poor circulation that develops during the day from wearing tight shoes or high heels. You can do both exercises sitting down, one foot at a time, or with both feet together. Remember to do these during the day when your feet feel cramped or tired.

STRETCHES

Stretching not only makes you more flexible and pliable, it increases the efficient strength of your properly stretched muscles. Though it does not plump up muscles, it does work to make them lean, strong and well defined.

A well-stretched body always creates the impression of longer lines, fluidity of movement and supple gracefulness. Dancers and karate practitioners move with beauty and assurance largely because they have extended their musculature with concentrated stretching techniques. Strength comes from relaxation, not from rigidity.

For positive attitudes and strength of mind and spirit, good stretching is essential. Almost everything we aim for in life requires us to stretch beyond our normal limits or out of familiar habits. Knowing our bodies are pliable—and often visualizing goals we wish to reach while we stretch in these exercises—helps us to feel secure in our ability to extend ourselves in personal and professional life situations. Superlife stretches are essential components of working the ensemble of mind, body and spirit.

RAG DOLL

Benefits: This increases circulation and stretches the lower back, hamstrings and legs.

Visualization: You are a rag doll. When you fold over, your shoulders and upper body are completely pliable. A good visualization is stretching to see your surroundings from every angle.

Breathing: Inhale deeply while standing up. Slowly begin to exhale from the abdomen as you bend, exhaling more completely as you relax, letting out still more breath as you pivot toward each side.

1. Separate your feet at slightly more than shoulder distance. Your arms are at your sides, your hands on your thighs, your shoulders relaxed.

2. Bend forward, keeping your back and shoulders relaxed but with your head straight forward, moving your hands down your legs. Count to 5, slowly.

3. Let your rag doll body fold all the way forward, relaxing your head and neck so they come as close to the floor as possible without straining. Keep your back flat so you go all the way over. If you can reach the floor, rest the backs of your hands on it. *Do not bounce*. Count to 5, slowly.

4. Keeping your hands together, gently bring your body toward your left leg. Try to look forward under your right arm. Count to 5, slowly.

5. Still keeping your hands together, slowly rotate toward your right leg. Try to look forward under your left arm. Count to 5, slowly. Then, return your head to the center, dropping it even further if possible, and count to 5, slowly. Slowly raise your body to the upright position.

Reps: Do the entire rag doll exercise 3 times, each time coming back to the starting position to begin again.

NOTE:
· *Do not bounce* in any position. Bouncing tends to overextend the stretch and may be the cause of pulled muscles. Extend the stretch by letting your body move naturally, without forcing it.
· If you have a weak lower back, keep your knees slightly bent throughout this exercise.
· Keeping a flat back will help you reach further down toward the floor and maximize the stretch on the backs of the thighs.

THE BRIDGE

Benefits: This is one of the best exercises for lower-back and spinal flexibility and relaxation. It also stretches the lower abdomen and legs.

Visualization: Your body is a bridge, leaning back to cover the distance behind you. Imagine "bending over backward" to get what you want most.

Breathing: Unlike all other Superlife exercises, with the Bridge you must hold your breath *in* during the maximum point of stress. Inhale very deeply, sucking your abdomen in tightly and pushing your chest up and forward as far as it will go. *Hold* your breath as you make the backward bridge. Exhale deeply as you straighten up again. Remember, it is important to hold your breath and maintain a tight abdomen and chest in this exercise to avoid straining your back.

1. Stand with your feet separated shoulder width apart. Place the palm of one hand on your solar plexus and the back of the other against the middle of your spine as you pull up your chest and abdomen on a deep inhale.

2. Make fists with both hands and push them hard against your upper buttocks on each side as you bend your knees slightly. Hold your breath and keep your chest up and out, your abdomen pulled in.

3. Make a bridge backward from the hips, pushing your fists hard against your buttocks. Hold your breath in. Exhale as you slowly straighten your body and let your arms hang down.

Reps: Do 5 back bridges.

NOTE: This exercise is wonderful for lower-back problems, providing you remember the following:
· Keep your chest held high and forward;
· Keep your abdomen held in tightly;
· Push hard against your buttocks with both fists as you bridge back, holding your breath.

ACCORDION STRETCH

Benefits: This expands, stretches and relaxes the body from head to toe.

Visualization: Your body is an accordion.
Breathing: Inhale deeply as you fold the accordion inward, exhale fully as you stretch it out.

1. Start on your hands and knees, with your head straight forward and your back straight.

2. Inhale as you simultaneously tuck your head down to your chest and raise your bent left knee in toward your head.

3. Now exhale and lift your head up and back while you straighten and raise your left leg back and up as high as you can. Return to starting position.

Reps: Do 10 reps of fold/stretch with the left leg (counting each fold/stretch movement as 1). Repeat with the right leg.

PUSHING THE FLOOR

(Push-ups from the Knee)

Benefits: This stretches and tightens all parts of the arms and prevents or reduces flabby skin in front of the armpit where the arm and chest come together.

Visualization: Visualize the floor rising and your need to keep it pushed down and away from you. You are pushing the floor away so you can continue to rise above things.

Breathing: Inhale deeply from the abdomen while you are up with your arms straight. Exhale deeply as you lower yourself to the floor and begin to push it away for the rise upward.

1. Start on your hands and knees. Your knees are slightly separated, your feet up in the air. Your back is straight, head straight forward. Exhale as you bend your elbows and lower your body down to the floor. Keep your back and neck straight.

2. Push the floor away as you rise up again. Once up, inhale.

Reps: This exercise, sometimes referred to as push-ups from the knee, should be done 10 times. After practicing, gradually work up to 20. If you can do this easily, then complete 2 sets of 20. However, if doing 10 is too difficult, start with 5 and gradually increase to 20.

Benefits: This stretches the lower back, hips, groin muscles and inner thighs. It also helps to increase kicking height.

Visualization: As you lower into a split (or whatever degree of it you can reach), visualize your pelvis detaching itself so your upper body rises away from the floor as your lower body moves down toward it.

Breathing: Exhale deeply as you exert the maximum stretch so that oxygen circulates to your lower body.

SPLIT AND STRADDLE
(Chinese Splits)

1. Stand with your feet wide apart and bend over to touch the floor with both hands for support.

2. Begin sliding your legs out, supporting your body with your arms and hands. As your heels slide out to the sides, your toes should be raised.

(continued on next page)

3

4

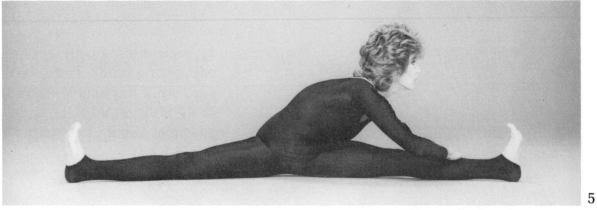

5

3. Slide out as far as you can to the point of tension. *(Control your movement carefully so as not to pull your groin muscle.)*

4. Lower your body to the floor, either by splitting completely or by sitting down. Keep your legs spread as wide as possible on the floor. Point your toes upward.

5. Keeping your back and head straight, pull your chest as close to your left knee as possible without straining. Count to 5, slowly.

6. With your back and head straight, pull your chest as close to your right knee as possible without straining. Count to 5, slowly.

7. With your head and back straight, pull your head and chest toward the floor in front, to point of tension, keeping your face forward. Count to 5, slowly.

Reps: Do 1 split and straddle 1 time to left, right and center to start. After you are able to split more comofrtably, increase stretching to 3 times each—left, right and center.

NOTE:
· If you are already able to split, the only caution is: *Do not bounce* when you straddle to either side or to the center.
· It is urgent to control your body as it lowers to the floor to avoid strain. Do not split on a slippery surface where your feet may slide out from under you.
· Do this exercise only to the point of tension. With practice and internal discipline, you will gradually be able to split wider and better.

TOUCHING THE CEILING WITH CHIN

Benefits: These cross-legged sit-ups tighten and firm the abdominal muscles and strengthen the upper and lower back.

Visualization: Attached to your chin is a string that tightens to pull you toward the ceiling so your chin will touch it.

Breathing: Inhale as you lie flat; exhale deeply from the abdomen as you pull up with your chin.

1. Start by lying on your back on the floor. Your right knee is bent with your foot flat on the floor. Your left knee is bent with your ankle resting on your right knee. Your hands are clasped behind your neck for support only, not to lift your head.

2. Inhale from your abdomen, and begin to exhale from your abdomen as the visualized string pulls your head up toward the ceiling with your chin leading. Push your bent left leg against your right knee. Continue to exhale as the string tightens to pull your chin and upper body further toward the ceiling, then slowly lower to floor. *Keep your back and neck straight.*

Reps: Do 10 to 25 of this exercise with your left leg off floor, then with your right leg off floor. As soon as you can, gradually increase to 2 sets of 25 on each side.

BALANCES

Balance—the ability to maintain and constantly recapture your equilibrium—is the basis for security in almost all physical activity as well as in daily living. Good balance can be developed by practicing a combination of movement, breathing and visualization.

In order to do this, it is essential to feel your own center. As you breathe and move, be aware of energy, action and relaxation emanating from the lower abdomen. This will help to make you feel rooted—not only physically in exercise but mentally and emotionally throughout everyday occurrences. Being well balanced and centered will give you an enormous sense of stability and resiliency; and it will provide you with a firm sense of self from which you can move out to be more effective at accomplishing tasks. Visualize yourself working all parts of your body in order to be balanced in any life situation that concerns you.

At the start of these exercises, you may need to hold onto a chair, counter or wall for support. Exhale deeply and re-visualize your rootedness when you feel wobbly. Then gradually begin to loosen your supporting arm to balance independently.

Extending both arms out fully to either side is a balance aid, as is focusing your eyes on one specific point. Eventually you will not need to extend your arms and will be able to do these balances with your eyes closed. Remember to first relax into your stance, no matter how your raised leg is positioned. As balance skill increases, you can work for higher leg positions and longer holding times.

PUSHING THE CEILING

Benefits: In addition to improving balance, this exercise will strengthen and stretch your arms, abdominals, upper thighs, calves and arches.

Visualization: In order to exercise dynamic tension in the musculature as you balance, visualize that the ceiling has come down and you must push it up with all the force and concentration your mind and body can muster.

Breathing: Inhale as you start the exercise, and keep exhaling to stay rooted as you push up the ceiling farther and rise onto your toes.

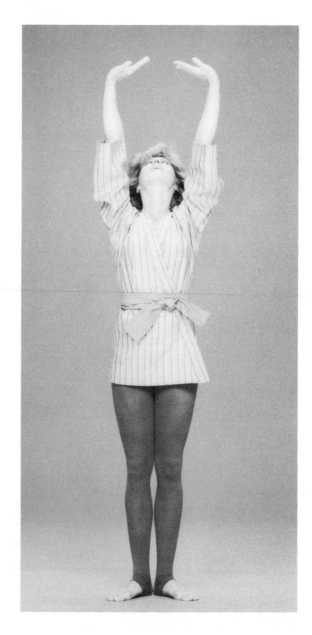

1. Stand straight, your feet together, arms at your sides. Inhale. Exhale as you raise your arms and begin to push the ceiling upward with the palms of both hands, as high as they will go.

2. Then raise up onto your toes and continue to push the ceiling upward. Return to the starting position.

Reps: Do 5 complete ceiling pushes, slowly. When your arms are straight up, count to 5, holding the position. Then, up on your toes, hold and count to 5 again.

THE STORK

Benefits: This enhances balance and tightens the inner and outer thigh muscles as well as the calves.

Visualization: Picture yourself as a stork (or flamingo), easily capable of standing firmly on one leg for long periods of time.

Breathing: Inhale and exhale slowly from your center, making sure to exhale deeply so you can feel the breath and energy moving into your legs.

1. Stand holding a counter or a chair with your right hand. Bend your right knee and grasp your toes with your left hand, lifting your right foot up until it rests against the front of your left thigh, sole upward.

2. Release your hand so that your foot stays up by itself, and make a fist at your waist with your left hand.

3. Gradually release your right-hand support, and make a waist-height fist with that hand too. Hold for slow count of 10 (increasing count to 20 as balance improves). Repeat standing on opposite leg.

Reps: Do one stork on each side, counting to 10 (and later to 20) once you are in position and have released your supporting hand.

NOTE:
· Release your supporting hand cautiously at first. As you relax, you will find it easier to do the stork without support.
· The fabric of some tights or dancewear is slippery, causing your foot to slide down your thigh. If that happens, try another type of fabric, or try it barelegged.
· Push your foot hard against your thigh with knee out and back so your legs lean against each other for balance.

MEDICINE BALL

Benefits: Maintained muscle tension tightens the arms, legs and back. Awareness of breathing and smooth movement enhances grace and balance.

Visualization: You are holding an extremely heavy medicine ball.

Breathing: Inhale and exhale from your center, slowly and deeply.

1. Stand with your feet a few inches apart. Turn your whole body slightly to the left, including your left foot with your toes turned slightly out. Your right foot also points out slightly, with your instep facing your left foot. Your arms are bent, as if holding a medicine ball close to your chest.

2. Very slowly push the heavy ball out in front of you while gradually shifting your weight onto your left (forward) foot. However, do not lift your right foot off ground.

3. Slowly pivot your upper body and the medicine ball toward the front, keeping your arms straight out in front and redistributing your weight so it is more even again.

4. Keeping your feet in the same position, gradually pivot your upper body and extended arms to the right, shifting your weight onto your right (rear) foot as you reach toward the right, bending your right leg slightly and straightening the left.

5. Pull the medicine ball back into chest as your weight redistributes evenly onto both feet. Repeat the entire exercise to the other side.

Reps: Do 1 slow rotation (side, front, other side and back) to each side, reversing your feet and weight distribution.

NOTE: Visualizing the enormous weight of the medicine ball is essential so that you will maintain tension in your arms and legs for firming and balance.

FRONT-KICK BALANCE

Benefits: This works balance skill, leg control, the lower back and the upper thighs.

Visualization: Visualize the single leg on which you are standing as a deep, healthy root, anchoring you firmly on the earth.

Breathing: Inhale and exhale deeply from your center, remembering that the last part of the exhale will help to stabilize you.

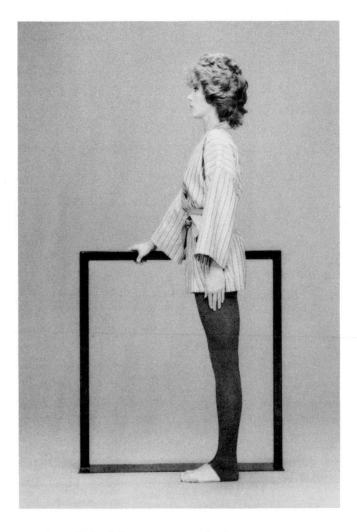

1. Stand, holding onto a chair or a counter with your right hand, your feet together, your left hand at your side.

2. Bend your left knee and, with your left hand, pull your knee up high toward your chest. Keep your toes straight forward and pulled up.

3. Release your left leg and extend it all the way forward. Remember to lead with the ball of your foot. Form an upturned fist with your left hand at waist height.

4. Gradually release the supporting hand from the chair or center and make a fist as you extend your right arm out in front of you, palm facing downward. Stand straight. Count to 5, slowly. (Increase count to 10 as balance improves.) Repeat the entire exercise to the other side.

Reps: Repeat 2 times with each leg.

NOTE: Keeping the ball of the front kick leading and the toes pulled back and up is what really makes this exercise tighten the upper thighs while honing balance skill.

BACK-KICK BALANCE

Benefits: By leading with the heel on a back-kick balance, the calves and the backs of the thighs become very firm. The lower abdominals and back muscles also get a workout.

Visualization: Use the same visualization as for the front-kick balance. Your supporting leg is a root that grounds you securely to the earth.

Breathing: Be sure to exhale deeply so your breath and energy flow down through the root. Maintain your center.

1. Stand holding a chair or counter with your right hand, your face straight ahead, feet together, your left hand at your side.

2. Make fist with your left hand at waist height. Simultaneously, bend your left leg and lift it behind you with the sole of your foot upward. Keep your foot flexed.

3. Extend your left leg all the way back, remembering to lead out with your heel.

4. Once your balance has stabilized, release your right, supporting hand, and extend your right arm all the way in front of you with your hand in a turned-down fist. Hold for count of 5, increasing to 10 as your balance improves. Repeat the entire exercise to the other side.

Reps: Repeat 2 times with each leg.

NOTE: Remember to push your heel out with your toes pulled up. This is what works the leg muscles to firm them.

SIDE-KICK BALANCE

Benefits: This is one of the best exercises we know of for tightening those outer triangles of flesh on the thighs—just below the buttocks—that tend to bulge on most women. But to make it work, you must lead out firmly with the outer ridge bone of your foot.

Visualization: Picture the same anchoring through the root of one leg supporting your centered body for natural stability.
Breathing: Breathe from your center and exhale deeply.

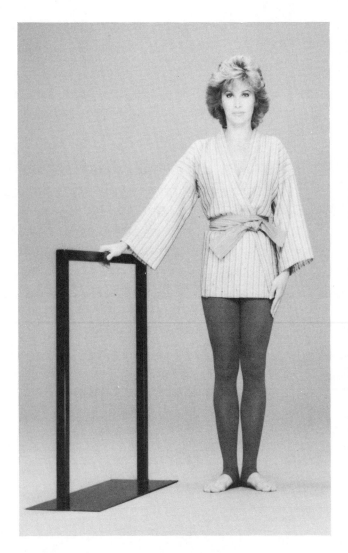

1. Stand with your feet together, your left hand at your side, your right hand holding a chair or a counter for support.

2. Bend your left knee and, with your left hand, pull your knee up and into your chest—near your armpit so it is positioned for side extension.

3. Extend your left leg straight out, holding it with your left hand for support as it extends fully. (If you prefer not to support your leg while it is extended, that is okay too). Remember to keep leading and stretching out with the outer ridge bone of the foot.

4. Try to stabilize your balance. Then release your supporting right hand from the chair, keeping your arm straight out for balance. Hold for count of 5, increasing to 10 as you secure balance. Repeat the entire exercise to the other side.

Reps: Repeat 2 times with each leg.

NOTE: Review the foot positions for the side-kick (see page 79). When the outer ridge bone and the ankle stretch out with the toes pulled up and back, you get the magic pull that tightens that small chunk of thigh where fat seems to go first.

PKA POWER TECHNIQUES

These power techniques, performed in repetitions and combinations of repetitions, will condition you aerobically; work your total body coordination; and give you strength, stamina and a feeling of well-being.

I am not a karate expert. The techniques taught here are the most basic ones used in karate. Learning and practicing them will not make you a karate expert. The benefits you will get from them, however, include a sense of centered movement and action, power, grace, mobility and an overall feeling of self-confidence. The techniques will enable you to move well through a variety of life situations with strength and ability.

You will also find that your weight will tend to drop and stabilize. However, weight loss and aerobic benefits will vary depending on the number of reps and the frequency of performing the techniques.

In most good karate classes, students do a sufficient number of technique reps to satisfy requirements for aerobic and cardiovascular fitness standards. Even if you do not use PKA techniques for complete cardiovascular satisfaction, performing them for approximately fifteen minutes three times weekly will aid your cardiovascular well-being.

If you have not studied karate, you may feel awkward at the start. Hand punches and thrusts cause unfamiliar feelings, especially for women. If you have had dancing experience, the most difficult thing will be to position your feet properly for kicking techniques. Dancing usually teaches you to point and reach out with your toes. Karate, for added power, muscle toning and foot protection, teaches you to position your feet differently. After working at it a bit, though, you will see amazing toning benefits from the hand and foot movements.

In time, the ability to make strong, decisive movements from a solidly centered, balanced, relaxed body will become habitual. Your speed and suppleness will increase; and you will lose almost all sense of being frail or "wimpy," both in movement and attitude.

The feminine yin and the masculine yang will begin to evolve harmoniously. As you work to feel comfortable performing the techniques, remember that you are simply enhancing whatever part of the yin-yang equation that has eluded you until now.

THE GI

In the techniques photos and elsewhere throughout this book I am wearing a karate uniform called the gi (pronounced "gee," with a hard "g" as in gain). Gi is the Japanese word for uniform. The trouser waist is usually drawstringed or elasticized, often both. The wrapped kimonolike jacket varies from just below the waist to hip length; and the pants can be midcalf, ankle length or anything in between. In a karate class or competition, the color of the belt indicates the practitioner's level of proficiency—black belt being the highest level. Gis are wonderfully comfortable for exercise or as sportswear for everyday activities from leisure time to business life (where a skirt can be substituted).*

*To order a white PKA gi and belt for exercise and sports wear, send $34.95 (includes postage and handling) to:

> PKA PRODUCTS—Superlife
> P.O. Box 10689
> Beverly Hills, CA 90213

Include your name, address, zip code, area code and telephone number (please print). Also enclose your height, weight, dress size and pant size.

REVERSE PUNCHES

Benefits: This sharpens your ability to focus and improves mobility and the speed at which you can move your arm and shoulder joints. Also, the gripping movement in the horse stance tightens the inner thighs.

Visualization: Select target marks on the opposite wall—one for your right hand, one for your left. Picture your fists whipping out to touch the marks, then snapping back like a towel. Move with strength of purpose.

Breathing: Breathe from your center but not as deeply as for slower exercises. Exhale as you punch out. On each exhale, be sure to open your mouth and push your breath out. To keep these short exhales centered, make a noise from the throat, uttering "hah" on each fast exhale.

1. Separate your feet shoulder-width apart. Bend your knees, keep your feet pointed slightly inward and a grip an imaginary horse with your inner thighs. Make a fist with your left hand and hold it out in front of you palm side down, with a bent elbow. Also make a fist with your right hand, palm side up, keeping your elbow bent and in close to your waist.

2. Extend your right fist forward as you turn it palm down for striking. Simultaneously, turn your left fist palm up as you pull it back, bringing your elbows in close to your waist.

1

2

3

4

5

3. Exhale as you punch out with your right fist, and snap it back.

4. Start reversing your hands by extending your left arm and turning it fist down while pulling your right arm back, fist up, and bending it close to your waist. Inhale during this transition.

5. Exhale as you strike out a punch with your left fist, snapping it back quickly.

Reps: Alternating left and right hands, do 20 reverse punches at three-quarter speed, then 20 at explosive speed.

NOTE:
· Remember, you are reversing only your arms, rolling your fists upward or downward. Reverse your fists as they meet about midway in front of you.
· Snap your punches out and back sharply. *Do not lock your elbow out.*
· Keep your buttocks tucked under.

BACK-FIST REPS

Benefits: This hones hand–eye coordination and speed of reaction. It also loosens shoulders and elbows, helps to adjust your focus rapidly and firm the arms.

Visualization: Select a target mark on walls to each side of you at shoulder height. See yourself pushing out the punches and snapping them back as though you could extend your power completely through the space of any room you occupy.

Breathing: Breathe from the abdomen, with a "hah" uttered from the throat each time you exhale and punch. This will keep you centered, balanced and powerful.

1. To begin, your feet are apart at shoulder distance, with your weight evenly balanced toward the forward part of your feet. Your elbows are bent, with your fists up, facing inward at chin height.

2. Raise your left elbow up and out to your left side. Turn your head to the left to see the target mark selected straight out from the bent left elbow.

3. Direct the full force of your energy through your left arm to your fist. Snap out your left fist to strike sharply with back of fist, snapping your elbow back as soon as it has reached full extension so that your fist is near your chin.

4. Raise your right elbow up and out to the right side and turn your head to the right to site the target mark.

5. Snap out a sharp right back-fist punch, pulling it back in immediately so your fist is near your chin.

Reps: Alternating your left and right hands, do 20 back-fists at three-quarter speed, then another 20 at explosive speed. When you become conditioned, increase to 30 reps at each speed, then raise to 40 at each speed.

NOTE:
· *Snap* your elbow; do not lock it out.
· At all speeds, do these moves properly with focus and power. Speed will increase with practice, and explosive speed will produce perspiration.

PALM-HEEL REVERSE PUNCHES

Benefits: Because of the palm-heel position, you may extend your elbow completely without risk of injury. This is a great exercise for tightening the upper parts of the arms, where sagging tends to occur. It also strengthens and elongates the back muscles.

Visualization: Visualize an opponent taller than you and on either side of you as target identification. Palm-heel strikes are also pushing stretches. Thus, it helps to visualize something or someone you wish to push away from yourself, so you will be freed of feeling closed in and restricted; or picture something you want and need to stretch out to get.

Breathing: Breathe from the abdomen, again uttering a "hah" from the throat as you exhale and strike out with your palm heel.

1. Your feet are apart at shoulder distance, with your knees slightly bent and gripping in a modified horse stance; your weight is evenly balanced. Your elbows are bent with your open hands held, palms up, near your hipbones.

2. Make a fist with your right hand, begin pushing your left arm forward with palm open and your fingers down. Simultaneously, twist your hips 45 degrees toward the right, shifting your weight onto your right (forward) foot, and raising your left (rear) heel from the floor.

3. Turning your left hand so fingers are up and bent at the joint, strike out forcefully to the upper right with your left palmheel. Return to the starting position.

4. Close your left fist and open your right as you begin twisting hips to the left, changing your weight balance.

5. Push your right hand completely across and up, turning it so the palm is open with the fingers raised to strike out powerfully with the right palm heel.

Reps: Alternating your left and right hands, do 20 palm-heel reverses at three-quarter speed, then another 20 at explosive speed. Raise the count to 30 at both speeds when you are conditioned, and then to 40.

BACK-FIST/PALM-HEEL REVERSE COMBINATIONS

Benefits: This increases hand—eye coordination and cardio-vascular circulation. It works balance and focus skills while toning and firming the arms (particularly the upper fleshy part), back and chest muscles. It also slims the waistline.

Visualization: Visualize as you did for the two preceding exercises, because here you will be combining both of those techniques.

Breathing: Breathe as in the previous two exercises, from the abdomen, quickly, by exhaling with your open mouth as you strike out and making a "hah" sound on the exhale.

1

2

3

4   5

1. Your feet are shoulder-distance apart, with your weight evenly balanced. Your elbows are bent with your fists up near your chin and your palms toward center.

2. Execute a snapping left-handed back-fist to the left.

3. As your left fist returns to your chin, swivel to the left and bring your right hand across to your left side for a forceful palm-heel strike.

4. As your right hand snaps back to your chin, swivel to your right side and back-fist to the right, snapping your right fist out and back.

5. Cross your open left palm over to your right side for a strong palm-heel strike.

Reps: Alternating left to right, do 10 combined back-fist/palm-heels at three-quarter speed, then another 10 at explosive speed.

NOTE:
· Remember to *snap* back-fists and *extend* palm heels.
· Stay focused on targets with all punches to each side.
· To begin, move with power and assurance. You can increase speed with practice.

FRONT SNAP KICKS

Benefits: This is great for firming leg muscles—it works all parts of the thighs and lower legs. It is also good for balance, focus, agility and honing foot—eye coordination.

Visualization: Visualize an opponent or target mark to kick out at. Keep your mark low to start, raising the height of your kicks as you progress. Because this kick is also a stretching—pushing movement, you can also visualize a life situation you want to stretch for or push away. But here you will use the lower half of your body to express those feelings. Remember, what you focus on mentally is transmittable to your entire body.

Breathing: Breathe from your abdominal center. Exhale sharply each time you kick. On the exhale, make a "hah" noise from the throat or push your breath out through pursed lips. Feel your exhale activated from the abdomen.

1. Begin with the basic stance, your feet apart at shoulder distance, your knees bent slightly. Your arms are straight down with your hands in fists at your sides, slightly out from body with palms down. Rotate 45 degrees to the left, shifting your weight to your left foot.

2. Bend your right knee and raise it up close in to your body. (Eventually, work to raise up your knee to solar plexus height.) Keep your right heel pulled back and up toward your calf. Keep your right toes flexed back and up toward your shin.

3. Extend your right foot with force, kicking with the ball of your foot, and *snap* it back quickly. Then lower your right foot to the floor, and repeat with your left foot.

Reps: Alternating left to right, do 20 kicks at three-quarter then do 20 more at explosive speed. (Speed will increase with practice.)

NOTE:
· *Do not overextend your knees* while kicking. This is called a front snap kick precisely because the snap gives maximum force while protecting the kicking knee.
· Remember to keep your foot properly positioned for the front kick. This protects the toes and also provides the tension that slims and firms all muscles of the legs and feet.

PALM-HEEL/ FRONT-KICK COMBINATIONS

Benefits: This works all the muscles of the upper and lower arms, the chest, waist, abdomen, thighs, calves, ankles and feet. It is great for balance, focus, agility and full body coordination.

Visualization: Select target or opponent marks for aiming palm-heel strikes on both sides, above eye level. Also select marks for front snap kicks on each side. Add the image of a person or thing you need to stretch toward—or wish to push away from—and you will feel your total power and energy being used.

Breathing: From your abdominal center, breathe with a sharp exhale on each palm-heel strike, as well as on each kick. Open your mouth to utter "hah" as you exhale and strike or kick out, or audibly push your breath out from your abdomen through pursed lips.

1. Stand with your knees slightly bent, your feet apart at shoulder distance. Bend your elbows, making fists with both hands. Pivot your upper body slightly to the left, positioning your left fist out in front of your face and keeping your right fist pulled in near your chin.

2. Pivot more to the left, shifting your weight to your left foot, raise your right heel off the floor, and forcefully thrust your right arm across to the left for a palm-heel strike.

3. Keep your right palm extended as you bend your right knee and raise it to your solar plexus or higher. (Pull your heel back and up toward your thigh, curl your toes back and up.)

4. Thrust your right foot out for front snap kick (remember to snap it back). Lower your right leg, pivot to the right and reverse the whole exercise.

Reps: Alternating left and right sides, do 10 combinations at three-quarter speed and 10 at explosive speed to start. Later, to 20 combinations at three-quarter speed and 20 at explosive speed.

NOTE: You will probably feel awkward when you start this combination. However, soon after, amazingly, you will begin to feel agile, graceful and powerful as you become familiar with the movements and transitions.

STOMP KICKS

Benefits: This tightens the abdominals and all leg muscles. It also lengthens the back muscles and enhances balance.

Visualization: Visualize an opponent or target mark to your left side and slightly behind you. You will be striking with the heel of your foot at a target at approximately shin height. This is not a high kick; instead, the heel aims low and hard as your upper body remains positioned away from the target for protection. Eventually raise the target mark to groin height.

Breathing: Breathe from your abdominal center, exhaling on the force of the kick through an open mouth (with a "hah" sound) or through pursed lips (pushing air out sharply from the abdomen).

1. To start, your feet are apart at shoulder distance. Knees bent slightly, your arms are down straight at your sides, hands in fists. (Your right hand can hold a wall or counter for support if necessary.)

2. Lift your left leg and bend that knee, cocking it across toward the right. Keep your left foot close to your right leg, with toes pulled up tightly.

1

2

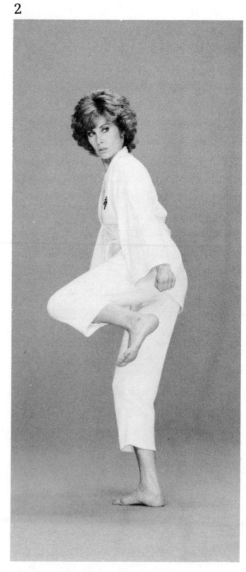

3. Lock out a stomp kick by striking with the back of your left heel. Keep posture upright, with left hip rolled slightly forward. Draw your foot back, bending your knee, and stomp out again for reps. Repeat with your right leg.

Reps: Do 10 stomp kicks slowly with your left leg, then do 10 at three-quarter speed with the same leg. Reverse, do 10 slowly with the right leg, then 10 more at three-quarter speed with the same leg.

NOTE:
· Hold onto a chair, counter or wall for balance when you start, working toward letting go as your balance improves.
· Remember to roll your hip forward for the stretch out and to keep your foot positioned properly, as this foot position is what allows you to stomp out the kick in a locked thrust without injury to the knee.

SIDE KICKS

Benefits: This is the best exercise for firming flabby thighs—and for working the fleshy area just beneath buttocks on the outsides of the thighs. For maximum effectiveness you must work hard to push out with that outer ridge bone of the foot.

Visualization: Visualize a target or opponent mark directly to each side. The side kick uses maximum leg stretch so you can also visualize reaching a goal as you perform it.

Breathing: As usual, breathe from the abdomen, exhaling as you make maximum extension on the kicks, with a noise to push the exhale out from your center.

1. To begin, your feet are apart at shoulder distance, your arms straight at your sides, hands in fists (or your right hand holding a wall or counter for support).

2. Bend your left knee, pulling it up toward chest and cocking it toward your right side. Keep your toes pulled back and up toward your shin.

3. Side kick to the left with your left foot, leading out with the side ridge bone of your foot. Direct your energy to that bone. Keep both legs straight, your toes curled up and back. Bend your left knee back in close to your body then kick again.

Reps: Do 10 slow kicks with your left leg, then 10 more at three-quarter speed. Repeat with your right leg.

NOTE:
· To start, hold onto something with your opposite arm for support.
· Pushing out with force and using the ridge bone of the foot will tone thighs like nothing else, as will holding the extension out at the farthest point, with power in movement.

COOPERATING EXERCISES

All Superlife exercises and techniques can be done alongside others in a karate class or with a partner at home. But there are some particularly effective stretching exercises that require both the participation and cooperation of another person.

Consider the difference between no-touch and touch dancing. When dancing or exercise partners do not touch, there is joint participation but not necessarily any cooperation. Both partners do their own routine at their own level. But in touch dancing, as in cooperating exercises, both partners must coordinate to produce one single effect.

This requires mental and physical sensitivity flowing between two people—a flow much like the best elements of cooperation in both our personal and professional lives. (This spirit is what has made working with my friend Robert Wagner on "Hart to Hart" so joyous.)

The Superlife Cooperating Exercises will help you focus on the value of shared experience; they will expand your ability to be aware of your responses to others and will help others become more sensitized to your responses.

Many of the notes on the following exercises are directed to the seemingly less-involved partner, because his or her action and interaction are the key to the doer's success. Though we each function independently in life, we must also rely on this formula for success in personal relationships and job efforts.

You can do the cooperating exercises with a woman, man or child. Most are interchangeable, but we have selected those for each pair that we have found work best in each situation.

In the first three exercises, I am cooperating with Bill "Superfoot" Wallace. Bill, who was the world's leading non-contact karate athlete, went on to become the PKA World Middleweight Champion. He held that contact karate title for six years and retired—undefeated after twenty-three challenges—in 1980. Bill tours throughout the world conducting clinics and seminars, and he is especially famous for his incredible stretching and kicking abilities.

In the next two exercises, I am cooperating with Judy; and in the final exercises I work with Ernie Reyes, Jr. By the time he was eight years old, Ernie had won every U.S. national title in forms competition. He was asked to stop competing with either children or teenagers because he continually outclassed them all. Forced to compete with adult forms heroes, he promptly became number seven in the nation—the only child in history to be nationally ranked in adult ratings.

Exercising in tandem often makes the hard work more fun. Exercising with a child helps the child to develop the habit of exercising young. These cooperating exercises help both children and adults to relax their egocentricity for the benefit of another or for common benefits from shared efforts.

WISHBONES
(On the Wall)

Benefits: This increases flexibility for kicking techniques and works on stretching the groin muscles as well as those of inner thighs.

Visualization: See your legs as wishbones, gradually separating to their maximum stretch, perhaps as one single line.

Breathing: Breathe from the abdomen, being sure to exhale deeply and thoroughly at the chief point of stretch.

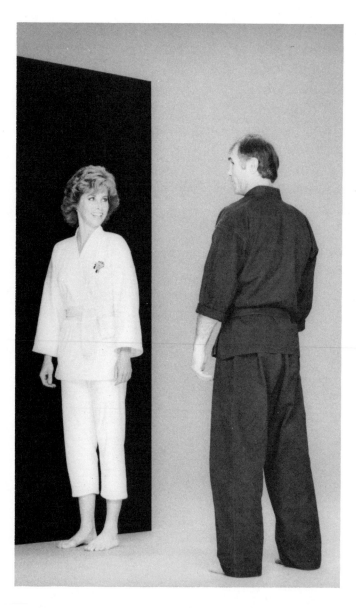

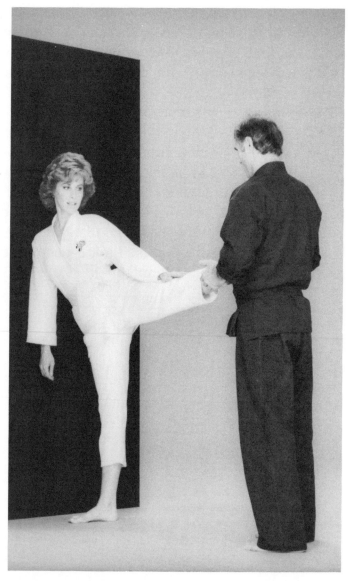

1. Stand erect, your right side to a wall.

2. Extend your left leg to the side and have your partner hold it firmly.

3. Have your partner begin to lift the leg, pushing it up toward the wall.

Reps: Both partners do 5 wishbones very slowly with each leg.

NOTE:

· Both partners must move very slowly and have patience while working for the stretched foot to reach the wall, gradually, over time.

· The stretching partner must tell the pushing partner when the point of tension has been reached.

· The pushing partner must not bounce the stretching partner's leg back and forth up toward wall.

4. As your partner pushes the leg to the maximum pressure possible, relax and continue to exhale. Allow your upper body to bend toward the floor while the wall supports you. Look up to your stretched foot. Repeat with your right leg; then reverse positions with your partner after reps to exchange roles.

WISHBONES
(Off the Wall)

Benefits: All leg muscles—particularly the thighs, hamstrings and groin muscles—will be well stretched with this exercise. The slow, focused movement here sharpens control and balance.

Visualization: Your body will become an expanded wishbone, with legs almost like the wings of gliders.

Breathing: Prolong deep exhales at the maximum stretch point, always breathing from the abdomen to avoid strain and to maintain balance.

1. The stretching partner faces forward and extends his or her right hand to the balancing partner's right hand for support. The balancing partner faces the stretching partner.

2. The stretching partner lifts his or her right leg waist high, and the partner holds the foot in his or her left hand.

3. The balancing partner moves backward, very slowly, as the stretching partner relaxes and exhales.

4. At the point of tension, the balancing partner stops and holds for 15 seconds. Increase this to 30 seconds with practice. Change legs; then partners reverse positions and roles.

Reps: Each partner should do 5 wishbones off the wall with each leg.

NOTE:
· It is important for both partners to remain interactive and sensitive to each another so that movement is very slow and controlled.
· The balancing partner must be awake and alert so as not to back up or drop too quickly. Try to actually feel your stretching partner's stretch.

LEG PUSHES AND SWINGS

Benefits: This works the waist, hips, groin, inner thighs, lower legs and ankles. Working from angles different than those of the wishbones increases mobility and flexibility as well as stretch.

Visualization: Visualize your legs and hips as elastic, able to be compressed and stretched with ease.

Breathing: Breathe from your abdominal center, with full exhales at the maximum pressure points.

1. Stand straight with your right side supported by a wall. The pushing partner faces you.

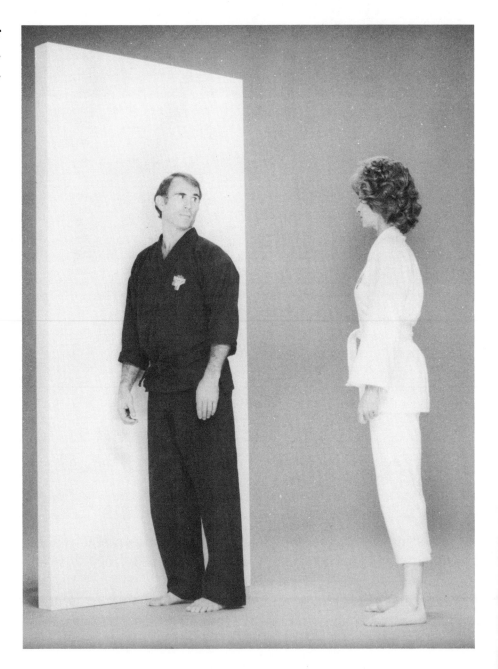

2. Extend your left leg sideways to the partner who supports it at waist height or higher.

3. Bend your knee as your partner pushes your leg toward the wall, in front of your left shoulder.

(continued on next page)

4. Try to slide your shoulder under your knee so your partner can bring your knee as close to the wall as possible.

5. Push your partner away from you with your left leg until it is straight out at your side, waist height to your partner.

6. Maintain balance against the wall as your partner "walks" your leg all the way around to the front.

7. Stay as erect as possible while your partner "walks" your leg all the way around to the rear. Change legs; then reverse the roles of the partners.

Reps: Each partner does 5 pushes and swings with each leg.

NOTE:
· To avoid knee pressure and strained groin muscles, have your partner stop pushing when the point of tension is reached. Stay erect.
· The pushing partner should neither push nor swing the leg beyond the point of tension.

SEESAWS

Benefits: This stretches the groin and inner thigh muscles and elongates the lower back muscles. It also develops strength and interactive awareness.

Visualization: Visualize your body as an elasticized seesaw, moving forward and backward with agility but very slowly.
Breathing: Keep your exhales long and deep from the abdomen at the maximum stretch.

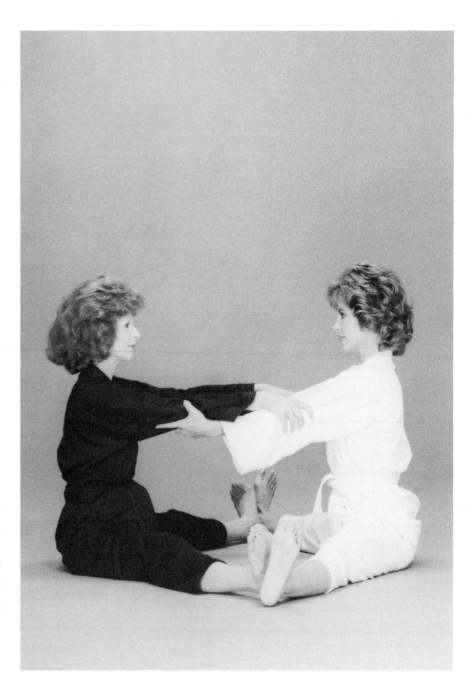

1. Both partners begin by facing each other on the floor, with their backs and heads erect. Both partners separate their legs as far as possible, one placing his or her feet against the ankles of the other partner. The partners hold their hands or arms *firmly*.

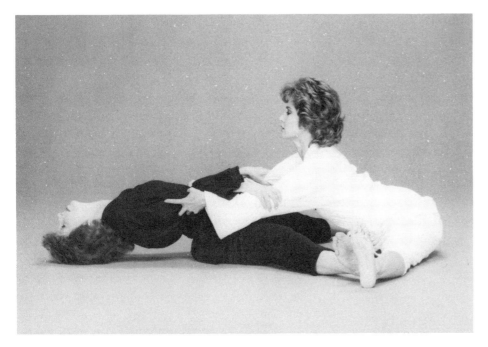

2. One partner starts lying back, "pulling" the other partner's upper body forward. Both should retain firm arm and hand support to maintain control. The partner going backward should push hard against the other's ankles at the same time. The partner going forward leads with chest, not head. Hold for count of 10 at the maximum stretch point.

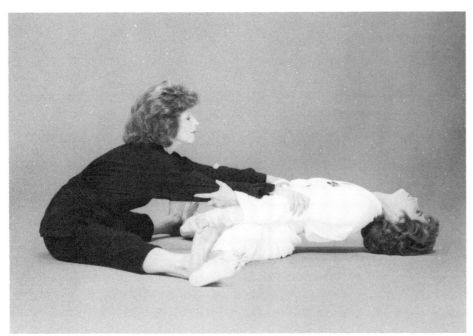

3. After returning to the starting position, reverse the direction of the seesaw.

Reps: Each partner should be pulled forward 3 to 5 times.

NOTE: It is important to cooperate so that the point of tension is not exceeded. This exercise stretches muscles that can be easily strained; thus, control is necessary. The supporting of arms, hands and ankles creates control factors for gradual movement.

BUTTERFLIES

Benefits: This exercise works the groin, inner thigh and lower back muscles, and elongates the upper back, sides and arms as well.

Visualization: Your body can swoop, stretched fully from side to side, like a butterfly soaring in the air.
Breathing: Breathe deeply from your abdominal center, with prolonged exhales at tautest stretch point.

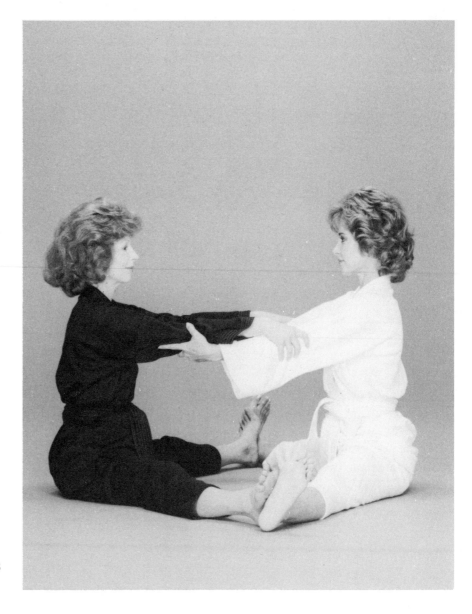

1. Start in the same position as for seesaws.

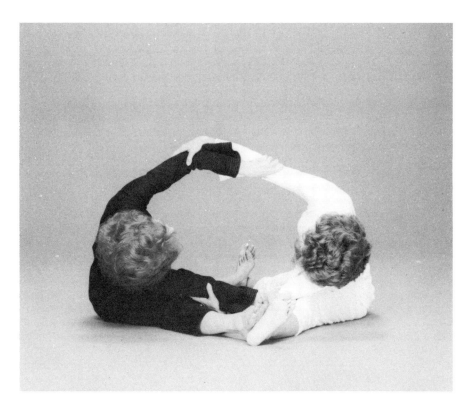

2. Partners bend at the waist to the same side, exhaling, and stretching as far to the floor as possible, keeping their backs and heads straight.

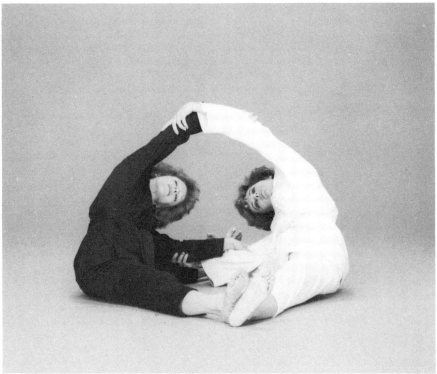

3. After returning to the upright position, the partners bend their waists and stretch to opposite side with their backs and heads straight.

Reps: Partners should do 5 butterflies in each direction, for total of 10 reps.

KICKING AROUND

Benefits: This stretches the leg muscles to enhance height for front kicks. It particularly works the hamstrings and also sharpens synchronization skills.

Visualization: Visualize a chorus line with you and your partner trying to raise the height of your kicks for performance.

Breathing: Inhale from your center for balance, exhale fully and quickly from your abdomen on the kick extension. Both partners should utter "hah" on kicks.

1. The partners face each other but stand about 2 feet to the side of one another. Both partners kick high, simultaneously, with the left leg and foot in the front-kick position (toes curled back and up to strike with the ball of foot).

2. Both partners lower the left leg and kick with the right leg.

Reps: Both partners kick 10 times with each leg for a total of 20 kicks.

NOTE:
· Test some kicks before starting to be sure you have allowed enough distance between you so as not to actually strike legs together.
· Each partner should establish his or her own height mark for a target, then hits it each time.
· Both partners establish a beat so their movements can be synchronized; and both keep the upper body straight while kicking.

PUSHED SPLITS

Benefits: This is a great hamstring stretch and wonderful for back and body alignment.

Visualization: Picture your body being able to separate at the groin so that, as in regular splits, your legs can separate to the fullest in either direction.

Breathing: The splitting partner exhales deeply and fully at the maximum stretch.

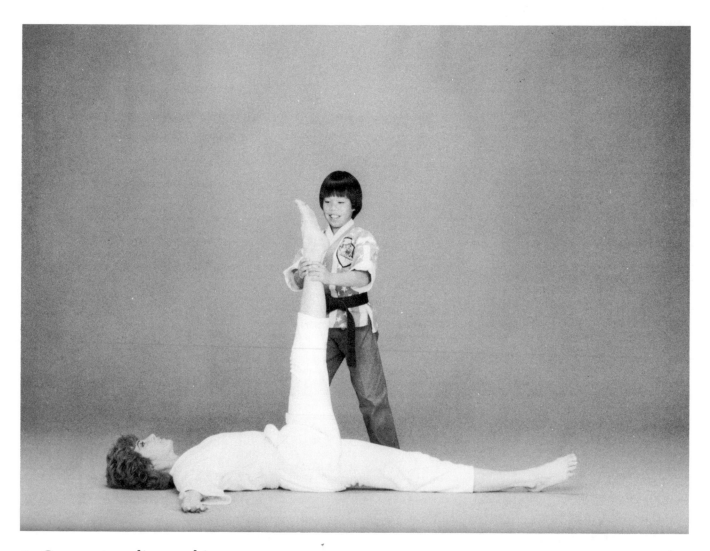

1. One partner lies on his or her back on the floor with the left leg pointing straight up. The pushing partner stands near the left leg, holding it high and straight.

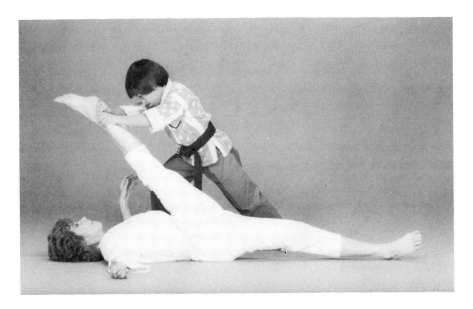

2. The pushing partner pushes the stretched left leg of partner back and above the head. The stretching partner keeps his or her body straight.

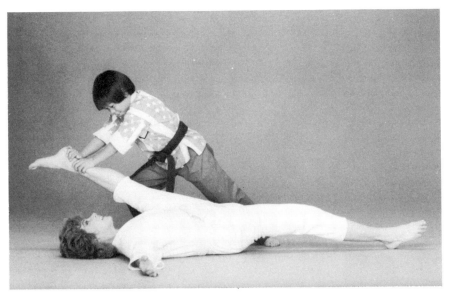

3. The pushing partner pushes the stretched left leg back toward the floor as far as the stretching partner can go and holds for count of 10. (Reverse legs, then reverse roles, so the pushing partner gets to stretch, too.)

Reps: Each leg of each partner should be pushed 5 times slowly.

NOTE:
· The stretching partner should keep his or her feet in a natural position.
· The partners should talk and interact to determine the maximum stretch point.
· The pushing partner should not bounce the stretching partner's leg up and down but should just push to the maximum tension point and keep the leg there for the count.

PANCAKES

Benefits: This stretches the inner thigh and groin muscles and loosens the ankles and tendons and ligaments in the knees and hips. It also improves the flexibility of leg muscles for kicking flexibility and foot positions.

Visualization: Visualize your legs as opposite sides of a pancake that keep flipping up as they are cooked. You must get the pancake sides to remain down, flat on the pan.

Breathing: Breathe from your abdominal center, making sure to give a maximal, deep exhale on the heaviest part of the stretch.

1

2

1. One partner sits on floor, with his or her knees bent and the soles of feet touching and held tightly together. The other partner stoops behind and presses the sitting partner's knees as close to the floor as possible.

2. Reverse roles and, if weight permits, have the lighter partner try making pancakes by standing on the sitting partner's thighs (barefoot of course!).

Reps: Start with 3 to 5 pancakes for each partner and increase to 8 to 10 with practice.

NOTE: If you want to stand on your partner's thighs or vice versa, *carefully* test this first to be sure your weight is not oppressive. It worked fine for Ernie, Jr., to stand on my legs, but clearly his smaller, lighter bones were not able to support my weight.

SUPERLIFE SLEEP

Just as there is a process in Superlife for gently waking into your day there is also a brief one for letting go of the waking hours so that you can easily give yourself over to the most relaxing sleep.

What keeps many of us from sleep—or causes us to sleep fitfully—is a carry-over of the day's stress. Many of us tend to fall asleep with our minds whirring, or perhaps we transport the day's problems into our sleep. Some people awaken in the middle of the night with charley horses in their calves. All of these things make the extraordinary healing qualities of sleep less effective.

In order to sleep soundly, we recommend doing the Run Away to Sleep exercise nightly, followed by a two-minute session of key breathing—all done on the bed. It works wonders for releasing stress; and Judy, who suffered sporadic nighttime charley horses in her calves for years, has never had another since doing this simple before-sleep routine.

If you need even more help with sleep, take a hot (not scalding) bath before retiring, and then do the exercise and the breathing. It also helps to rotate your head (as in the Head and Neck Stir of Joint Rotations, page 91) to release mental tension and to let energy move down into your body.

Remember, you cannot actually do anything while you sleep—except to treat yourself to a glorious, healing rest time. You deserve it . . . so relax, let go and enjoy.

RUN AWAY TO SLEEP

Benefits: This releases tension, relaxes the lower back and leg muscles, and allows energy to move down out of the head to end adult, rational "brain work" for the day.

Visualization: See yourself as a child. You've spent the whole day being as responsible an adult as possible. It is perfectly acceptable, even desirable, to allow yourself to feel like a child for this moment. Visualize your child self, longing for total freedom from responsibility, running away from all cares and even shaking your head to say "no, no, no" to any thoughts or concerns that would try to invade your joyous peace.

Breathing: It is important to breathe deeply from the abdomen, exhaling fully as you do the entire exercise. Inhale with your mouth closed loosely and exhale long and full with your mouth open, sighing out loud with pleasure during the release. Give a big sigh, all the way out, at the conclusion.

1. To start, lie on your back on the bed, with your knees raised and relaxed and feet separated. Your arms are at your sides, with your elbows slightly bent and your palms down. In this position, take 5 prolonged key breaths with good, deep exhales, feeling energy leave your head and travel down through your pelvis and lower body. Be sure your lower back is loose so there is no arching.

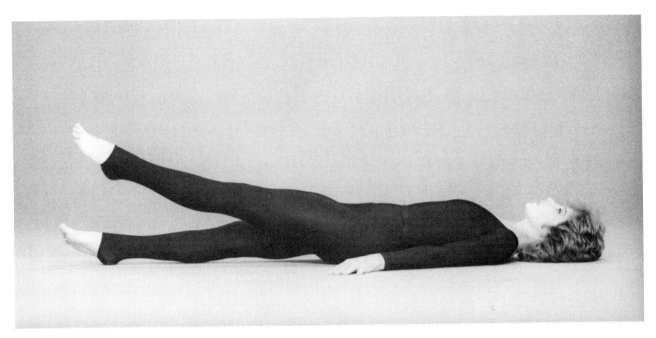

2. Straighten your legs out on the bed and, alternating left and right, raise one leg, then the other, as though you were running away to sleep. As you run, shake your head from side to side, saying or thinking "no, no, no." Give a big, relaxed sigh at the conclusion of the run. Resume the key breathing position with the knees up. Stay in contact with your breath and body for 2 minutes of relaxed key breathing.

Reps: Shake your head and run away fast for 10 to 15 seconds, then sigh all the way out. If you feel like it, repeat for another session of 10 to 15 seconds or more.

NOTE:
· Run fast and hard to get away to sleep. Your head won't shake from side to side as fast as your feet can run. Hit the bed with your heels only.
· If you share your bed with someone who is already asleep, do this exercise on a sofa or other soft surface, never on a hard floor.
· Whether alone or sharing your bed with someone, you will probably feel foolish doing this exercise. It is beneficial to lose such a self-conscious feeling by realizing that it is more important to get a good night's sleep than to create any type of impression. Presumably, a person who shares your bed is someone who cares for you and wants you to feel good and sleep well. Perhaps your partner will also be inspired to try this. Happy dreams to one or both of you!

PART IV

ADVANCED SUPERLIFE Kata

THE FLOW AND FORM OF KATA

Kata (pronounced "kahtah") is the Japanese term for the prearranged, dancelike exercise forms used in karate. These forms are comprised of the very same techniques practiced for exercise, self-defense and sparring. In kata, however, the techniques are woven into a preestablished, formalized pattern resembling a dance routine. Choreographed kata is made up of offensive and defensive movements, all of which may also be used in a self-defense situation. When these movements are performed to music, kata becomes a strong and magnificent form of dance.

The kata forms given here contain only those few basic karate techniques you have already learned, plus a simple four-corner block shown at the start of this section. We call it Advanced Superlife because it should be started after you feel comfortable with basic PKA techniques.

As each movement in the kata is also a self-defense move, there are two accompanying photographs for every kata step. In the first photo, you will see me performing the movement alone, as a step in the kata routine. The second photo shows how I can use that same movement against an attacker for self-defense purposes. The "attacker" in these photographs is Ernie Reyes, Sr., leader of the West Coast Demonstration Team, winner of every national group forms award in the United States as well as in several foreign countries. Additionally,

Ernie Sr. has been awarded the Black Belt Hall of Fame Award for instructor of the year, having taught numerous kata champions including his own son, Ernie Reyes, Jr.

At first, we must simply learn the steps of the kata just as we would memorize the steps in a dance routine. If you already know the few techniques utilized (from PKA Superlife Techniques practice), this will come more easily. Second comes the most difficult part of kata, learning to make smooth transitions between one movement and the next. To develop this sequential flow, use the visualization dancers use: See the routine in your mind's eye and "walk" through it. "Walking" through a routine means not performing it fully, merely indicating the movements with your body, hands or feet as you "play" it on your mental television set to visualize it.

The third phase is to empower and perfect your execution of the routine. To do this, you can use two types of visualization: the one that directs your own energy to the parts of your body utilized for the movement, and the one that sees the attacking opponent as the target of each move. And, finally, you will discover that when you practice the kata, a change of your attitude while performing it will alter the interpretation. When that happens, your own creativity takes over!

This last, creative phase is what distinguishes kata champions. For while they execute extremely complicated routines in competition, they always practice the basics as well. And it is their individual interpretation of even the basics that makes them champions. Kata has been likened to a "moving meditation," because its possibilities are as limitless as those of the human mind and spirit and become visible through the movement of the body.

As students advance in karate class, they are required to invent their own kata. At its best, these personal inventions resemble glorious spider webs of motion designed by creative people weaving layer upon layer of design and detail into space. It is quite breathtaking.

Yet even the basic kata forms given here offer the full benefits of the kata experience. What are those benefits? Almost everyone in the arts agrees that kata is more than technique, memory, smooth transitions and self-defense. It is also the total balance of yin and yang, the confluence of grace and power, of stretch and flex, of speed and stillness, and of mind, body and spirit.

Benefits: This improves circulation and focus and provides a sense of directional approach for any movement in a self-defense situation. It also tones the upper and lower arms.

Visualization: Visualize yourself standing in front of a large frame. You want to block, by pushing away firmly with your palms, any motion that might come toward you from any of the frame's four corners. Learn the moves, then really energize your arms and palms forcefully when you make them.

Breathing: Breathe from your abdominal center, being sure to exhale thoroughly as you push out with each block.

FOUR-CORNER BLOCK
(A Kata Technique)

1

2

1. Take a basic fighting stance, with your feet separated at shoulder distance, your head and upper body turned slightly to your left. Your elbows are bent and your hands are in fists, your palms facing toward the center at chin height.

2. First, block to the bottom left corner. Open your left fist, keeping your fingers straight (except for your thumb, which should be crooked and close to your hand). Make a sweeping motion with your palm, down and back, to push away an attack.

(continued on next page)

3. Resume your fighting stance (both fists up), then repeat the down block to the lower right corner, using your right hand.

4. Resume the fighting stance; then to block the upper right corner, open your left fist and push it across in front of your face to push away an attack coming from the upper right.

5. Resume the fighting stance, then open your right fist and push the block across your face to left side to block an attack from the upper left.

Reps: Repeat the entire four-corner block 10 times.

NOTE:
· The first two movements are called down-blocks because you are blocking by exerting force downward. The last two are called push-blocks because you are pushing off to the side to block.
· Directing strong energy into your blocking/pushing movements helps to tighten the fleshy part of the upper arms and strengthen the lower arms, hands and wrists.

INSTRUCTIONS TO ACCOMPANY KATA

Visualization: Each step of the kata has its own self-defense visualization. Each step also has two photos, one solo photo showing the form of the step, the second partner photo showing the focus and power of the self-defense visualization.

Breathing: All breathing for kata should be centered from the lower abdomen. When the movement is rapid, inhale and exhale more quickly. Prolong your breaths on slower movements. The pacing of the moves and their accompanying breaths is your choice.

Reps: It is very confusing to count reps while doing kata. Instead, each Part of the kata has its own information (under Reps) as to how much time you should allow for its practice or the practice of two or three Parts combined.

NOTE: Once you've learned the steps, try practicing kata at differing speeds and with changing attitudes. This is what makes kata feel more like interpretive dance. You can use different kinds of music to create varying moods. But if you feel awkward at first, be patient. Time and investment will reap joyous rewards. (Sounds like a fortune cookie, doesn't it?)

KATA: PART ONE

(Down-Blocks, Front Kicks, Reverse Punches)

Each step is depicted in a solo photo and is also shown with its own visualization in an accompanying photo.

Formal Stance: Each time you begin or end your practice of kata, take the formal stance shown in the large photo at the start of Advanced Superlife: Kata. Stand erect, your feet apart at shoulder distance, arms down in front of you, hands in fists, palms toward your body.

1

1. Swivel your body to the left, bending your elbows so your left fist is out in front of face and your right fist is near side of chin. (Visualization: You prepare for an attack coming from your left.)

Visualization

Visualization

2. Open your left fist and down-block to your lower left. (Visualization: You down-block to avoid a front kick coming at you from the lower left.)

Visualization

3. Bend your left elbow and re-form your fist again as you slide your right (rear) foot up to your left (front) foot. (Visualization: You prepare to avoid a grab from the left side.)

Visualization

4. Shift your weight to your right foot, raise your left leg and snap out a front kick at stomach or groin height. (Visualization: You use your leg and foot to distance yourself from the attacker.)

(continued on next page)

5. Return your left foot to the floor and distribute your weight on both feet for a fighting stance. (Visualization: Position yourself for a follow-up move.)

Visualization

6. Shift your weight onto your left (forward) foot, as you punch a right reverse punch with your right hand, keeping your left fist at your chin. Snap the punch to avoid elbow injury (Visualization: You simultaneously strike and distance yourself from the opponent.)

Visualization

7. Return to the fighting stance as you pivot to the right. Perform steps 1 through 6 to that side: down-block with your right palm; slide your left foot up to your right foot; front kick with your right leg; reverse punch with your left fist. (Visualization: You prepare to defend against an attack from the right.

Reps: Don't split your concentration by trying to count reps. Allow 5 minutes to repeat Part One to the left and right sides as described. To start, work on just the first three or four steps until they become automatic, then add the next few steps. Practice all steps to the left side until you're comfortable. Then practice them to the right. Once you've learned Part One, 5 minutes will mean approximately 20–25 reps of the entire Part.

NOTE: When practicing Part One only, take the formal stance at the conclusion of each practice, then bring your feet together and bow. When continuing on to Part Two, omit the stance and the bow here and proceed on to the first step of Part Two.

KATA: PART TWO

(Push-blocks, Reverse Punches, Front Kick, Left and Right Punches)

Take the formal stance if you are starting your practice here. If you are continuing from Part One, proceed from its last move to step 1 below.

Visualization

1. Pivot to the left, your elbows bent, your fists raised in a fighting stance. (Visualization: You position yourself for another attack from the left.)

Visualization

2. Take a full step forward with your right (rear) foot, so it is in front of your left foot, and push-block with your right palm pushing across, in front of your face, to the left side. (Visualization: You defend against the opponent's right-hand attack.)

Visualization

3. Bring your right hand back to your chin in a fist, and snap a reverse punch out with your left fist. Shift your weight onto right foot, with your left heel off the floor, to get power in the punch. (Visualization: You distance your opponent with an offensive strike.)

Visualization

4. Step forward with your left foot placed in front of your right as you push-block with your left palm across, in front of your face, to the right. (Visualization: You push away a left-handed punch.)

(continued on next page)

5. Bring your left fist back to your chin, shift weight onto your left (forward) foot, and snap out a reverse punch with your right fist. (Visualization: You strike to the opponent again, preventing his or her approach.)

Visualization

6. Bending your right elbow, bring your right foot up to snap out a front kick. (Visualization: You aim this kick at the opponent's groin, midsection or neck, as shown.)

Visualization

7. Drop your right foot down in front of your left and snap a right-handed punch at chin height. (Visualization: You knock the opponent back.)

Visualization

 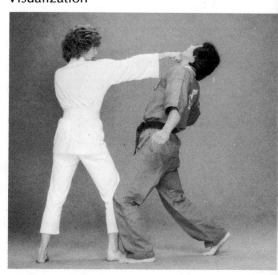

Visualization

8. Shift your weight completely forward onto your right foot, lifting your left heel off the floor, and snap out a left-handed punch at chin height. (Visualization: This left-handed punch, when it immediately follows a right-handed punch, as in step 7, is called a double punch. Feel the power of the two combined and coming quickly, and see the target on which their impact is directed.)

Reps: Practice Part Two for 5 minutes. This will mean approximately 25 reps, but don't try to count them. For an additional 5 minutes, practice Parts One and Two together. This means 10–12 reps of the two Parts combined, and a total of 10 minutes of kata practice.

NOTE: If you are concluding your practice here, take the formal stance, then bring your feet together and bow. If you are continuing to Part Three, omit the stance and bow and move on to the first step of Part Three.

KATA: PART THREE

(Back-fists, Side Kicks)

Take the formal stance if you are starting your practice here. If you are continuing from Part Two, proceed from its last move to step 1 below.

Visualization

1. Putting your weight on your left foot, bring right foot back so it's parallel with your left, facing forward. Then, looking to the right, cross your closed right fist *in front of* your open left palm, at chin height. (Visualization: You reposition again for another attack from the right side.)

Visualization

2. Step to the right with your right foot, and snap a right-handed back-fist to the right. (Visualization: You block an attempt to grab by back-fisting to the head or temple.)

Visualization

3. Sliding your right foot in next to your left foot, open your right hand and cross it *behind* your left fist. (Visualization: You are preparing to switch your defense to the left side now.)

Visualization

4. Step to the left with your left foot, and snap a left-handed back-fist to the left. (Visualization: Again you block an attempt to grab by back-fisting to head or temple.)

(continued on next page)

5. Leave all your weight on left foot, look to the right, and raise your right leg for a side kick to the right, leading with the outer ridge bone of your foot. (Visualization: You distance yourself with the ridge bone striking to opponent's stomach.)

Visualization

6. Lower your right leg, bringing your right foot near your left, keep your fists up near your chin and look to your left. (Visualization: Once again you prepare for a left-handed assault, focusing on the target.)

Visualization

7. Shifting all your weight to right foot, side-kick to the left with your left foot. (Visualization: Again you have distanced and used the outer ridge bone of the foot to strike at the stomach.)

Visualization

8. Bring your left leg down in front of your right foot, facing forward. (There is no visualization here, but you would now be ready to defend against an attack from the front with other kata moves designed for that purpose.)

Reps: Practice all of Part Three for 5 minutes. Once these steps are learned, practice all three kata Parts combined for another 10 minutes, or a total of 15 minutes of kata practice.

NOTE: For the closing formal stance of the kata, bring your right foot back, parallel to the left, and drop your arms and fists down in front of you. Then bring your feet together and bow.

PART V

SPARRING AND SELF-DEFENSE

SPARRING AND KARATE CLASSES

We have not included in Superlife any instruction related to the valuable sparring aspect of karate. That is because sparring can only be properly learned in an actual karate class. Nobody—men, women or children—should spar without simultaneously learning control under proper supervision. It takes a concerned, watchful instructor to teach control and to supervise how effectively each sparring partner exercises his or her mental and physical control in a match or practice session.

Sparring is an unpalatable concept for many women. But learning how to spar and doing it in a karate class is one of the greatest consciousness-raisers of all times, especially for female students.

Most women are brought up to think of themselves as delicate and breakable, both physically and emotionally. Many of us recall that we were told as children: "Be careful, you'll get hurt." In the meantime, the little boys we played with were encouraged to play harder but "not to hurt the girls." Too many girl children grow into womanhood (even today) believing they are made of glass, thinking of themselves as "breakable."

The PKA power techniques in Superlife will help women to feel more healthy, self-assertive and somewhat less breakable. However, there is nothing like a properly supervised sparring match to dispel the breakability myth forever and ever. Amen!

Both partners wear protective equipment on their hands

and feet. This safeguards their own striking surfaces as well as the targets of the partner's body. In the beginning, absolutely no contact is permitted in sparring. This is what teaches and hones control. For those students who rise in belt level through testing (many do, while others continue in class just for the workout), some *controlled* contact to certain areas of the body may be allowed. Contact to more vulnerable target areas remains outlawed. But protective gear assures that even if one partner slips, or ducks into a strike or kick, the blow will be cushioned by the thick padding of the gloves or footpads. (Judy and I are wearing protective gear in the photos. The footpads are not flattering, but they are welcomed as protection.)

Sparring partners—whether of the same sex or not—both learn a number of valuable things about themselves and each another. And both gain a new, special respect for themselves and for others as well.

First, for women, it is great to know you will not crumble into fragments—either emotionally or physically—when a punch or a kick comes at you. Second, you cannot help but accept your self-assertiveness in a new and healthy light. It becomes clear—to mind, body and spirit—that you can assert yourself for a specific purpose or goal and not lose control of your aggression. Thus you really learn self-regulation. It also becomes clear that other people have their own assertiveness and that a controlled sparring match is a miniversion of life itself.

When this process occurs between male and female partners, it is the best kind of training ground for more gratifying male/female partnerships, personally and professionally.

One note of caution: A great many women karate students (aged from five to sixty-five) develop "crushes" on their male instructors or more advanced sparring partners. As Judy explains it:

For many women, sparring represents the first time a strong, proficient and often attractive man has treated them as an equal. Many of these men are fine karate athletes with powerful, graceful bodies. They make demands on a woman, but the demands are intended solely to increase her own strength and internal power. This can be an enormously seductive experience for women who have consistently been underrated or "kept in their places" by men they have previously known socially and professionally.

Like most other types of instruction, there is both good and bad to be found in every style of karate.

There are now more than 7,500 karate schools throughout the United States, with countless others in countries around the world. If you would like a referral to a qualified school in your area, you can write to:

PKA Karate, Associated Schools Program
P.O. Box #10689
Beverly Hills, CA 90213

The organization will let you know if there is a PKA school in your locale, or another school with a good reputation.

When selecting a karate school, the style of karate is less important than certain other factors. First, find out how long the school has been in business. Then try to talk with students who have been there for a while. Check the hours and location of the school to discover if the geographical area and class hours work for you. Watch a class to see if a well-rounded curriculum is taught at the beginner's level.

Observe whether the instructor gives personal attention to the students with regard to class size. An instructor should also be firm about discipline and respect but not without earning respect by his or her own behavior.

Do not go to a class where an instructor has such an inflated "master" complex that he or she manipulatively belittles students. Even seasoned karate teachers are human beings; and respect is a two-way street.

Some schools make contractual agreements with students. If the school is reliable, a contracted program is, in the long run, a better buy and an easier arrangement for both the school and the student. Be sure the school is kept clean, even though it may be a relatively humble structure. Most important, see and feel the students' enthusiasm. Good teachers are the same everywhere. They generate enthusiasm and cooperation.

One last observation about sparring for women. It helps them to lose the type of "victim vibes" so often discussed in assaults of one type or another. Losing those "victim vibes" becomes, in and of itself, a great self-defense technique.

COMMON SENSE FOR SELF-DEFENSE

Most women do not even like to think about the need to protect themselves from physical danger. Judy and I do not think about such matters day and night, nor should you become paranoid about your safety. But statistics show that it is useful to know how to avoid trouble and what to do if it seems unavoidable.

Though we have shown you how the PKA Power Techniques you practice as reps can be used for both kata and self-defense, we would not advise you to presume you have truly learned to defend yourself until you have studied those techniques, and others, in a karate class that includes self-defense in its curriculum. It is important to practice with a partner who knows how to simulate a real assault, under the guidance of a professional instructor. Only in that way can you sharpen and test your responses, speed and power. And only after that process can you properly assess which defenses are best for you in any real-life situation.

There are, however, two useful lists that follow: one with advice that can help to prevent trouble, the other with actions you can take if trouble starts.

PREVENTIVE MEASURES AT HOME OR IN A HOTEL

· **Keep doors and windows locked.** Judy locked her glass door in a northern California hotel room one night, even though she wanted fresh air and saw that her second-story balcony led nowhere. At about 5 A.M., an armed robber got up onto her balcony and, finding her door locked, robbed the room next to her instead.

· **Always change locks immediately if you lose your house keys.**

· **Do not open your door to strangers.** Install a peephole or chain lock. If a salesperson or service representative appears without being summoned, call the company first before letting him or her in. If a stranger needs a phone for car problems or for any other purpose, make the call for him or her.

· **Do not presume that women strangers are harmless.** A woman "salesperson" robbed my friend at gunpoint in her home; and Judy's daughter and friends were mugged by a group of teenaged girls who also beat the group of friends with umbrellas.

· **Be conscious of what may prove to be warning signals.** Warning signals include obscene phone calls, hang-ups on the phone, strangers in the neighborhood, strange cars near your home or anything you can see or intuitively sense as strange when you open the door to enter your home.

PREVENTIVE MEASURES ON THE STREET

· **Be alert and aware as you walk.** Do not look frightened or dart your eyes all around, but do use peripheral vision and be aware of your surroundings and those who share the street.

· **Walk confidently and stay centered.** You will not "smell" like a victim to a would-be mugger.

· **Don't flaunt your valuables.** Muggers like valuables.

· **Avoid unsafe areas if you can.** They are surefire danger risks.

· **Walk near the curb at night.** Unseen trouble can be lurking in doorways.

· **Don't take shortcuts.** Alleys, fields and other isolated areas are unsafe.

· **Do not get into strangers' cars.** Doing so puts you at their mercy.

· **Be a sensible "Good Samaritan."** If you see someone in trouble, call or go to get help. The person who seems to be in trouble may be staging a setup for trouble of your own.

· **Have your keys ready to let you in.** This is sound advice—whether you are coming home or entering a car.

PREVENTIVE MEASURES IN CARS

· **Do not carry house keys on the same ring as car keys.** It makes them easy to steal; and parking attendants have been known to make copies of house keys.

· **Keep the doors locked when you are in the car.**

· **Keep the windows high enough so nobody can reach in to grab you.** This will prevent anyone from reaching in to open your lock or to grab something from you or off of you. (A friend of ours recently had her necklace and earrings pulled from her body while waiting for a stoplight at a busy intersection.)

· **Park for protection, even in the daytime.** Stay away from isolated parking spots. At night, try to park under a light or in a well-lighted area.

· **Look into the back seat before entering a car.** It does no good to get in and then look.

· **Do not leave your car for assistance in a secluded area.**

Highway patrols warn male and female drivers to leave a disabled car only long enough to tie a white piece of material on the antenna. Carry a handkerchief or something white in your glove compartment for this purpose. Then stay inside your car with windows and doors closed and locked until aid comes.

One final note related to cars. Judy and I wish it were not a requirement of the law to carry one's automobile registration in the car. Registrations have your address written on them, making it easy to follow or find you. Perhaps the registration forms could be changed so that addresses were not on the section to be kept in the car. If you feel as we do, get your friends to write letters to your State Department of Motor Vehicles.

COMMONSENSE TIPS FOR THE HOME, THE STREET AND THE CAR
(What to Remember if Approached by an Attacker)

· **Keep your distance.** The instant you feel a potential threat, try to gain distance from its source. Run away or step away first and then run, if you can. Step behind a short or tall object on the street, such as a garbage can, lamppost, car—whatever is available.

· **Scream "Fire" to yell for help.** Many people will respond to a cry of "Fire" who would otherwise avoid entanglement in a different sort of crisis. Your first priority is to get someone else to appear, regardless of what pretext you use to do that.

· **Give up your "valuables" to an armed robber or mugger.** We have put the word valuable in quotes, because your only truly meaningful possessions are your health and your life. Protect them—at all material costs. Cooperation from you can relieve an attacker's tension.

· **Don't appear fearful.** Try to keep your eyes and face expressionless. Attackers are often seduced by fear and become belligerent when challenged. Neutrality is the one thing that baffles them most, because it gives them nothing to feed on.

· **Use everyday objects as weapons.** According to the law, you may use a weapon only to defend your life. Even an everyday object can disfigure or kill, so be very sure you are in physical danger before using any of the objects listed here.

You may mean only to startle and to deflect an attack, but if you cause more serious damage, you may have to defend your action in a court of law. If, however, your physical person is endangered, the items listed below can be used for protection:

- **Perfume or hair-spray atomizers** can be sprayed into an attacker's eyes.
- **Keys** can be used as a weapon in two ways: holding one or more between your fingers sticking out from your knuckles in a fist, or a group of keys on a ring can be swung at an attacker's face or eyes.
- **Purses**, especially if they contain heavy objects, can be used to hit someone. But don't swing a purse at an attacker; he or she can easily grab your "weapon" away when you swing it.
- **Umbrellas** can be directed to an attacker's face, groin or other sensitive area.
- **A handful of coins** can be hurled at an attacker's face, and one coin held between your knuckles and protruding from your fist works nearly the same as a key.
- **Cigarettes, matches and lighter** are all weapons. A lighted cigarette in the face often stops an attack; a lighted book of matches can be thrown to create distance, and a cigarette lighter held in a fist weights the fist, making it more of a weapon. (This is the only instance in which anyone could possibly say that smoking might be good for your health!)
- **Loose face powder** can be thrown into the eyes.
- **A tightly rolled magazine or newspaper** can be used as a bat.
- **All pointed objects such as pens, pencils, eyebrow pencils, and the pointed handles of combs and eyeglass stems** can be used to jab the face or eyes.

· **Observe your attacker.** Your only chance to have an assailant punished by law is to remember what he or she looks like so you can make an identification. Try to observe age, height, weight or build, skin color, hair color and style, speech distinctions and any distinguishing physical characteristics such as shape of nose, color of eyes, scars, beards, mustaches and so on. Though it is difficult to be aware under pressure, it will be most advantageous to know what your assailant looked like.

PART VI

SUPERLIFE ENHANCERS

Over the years, most people develop beneficial personal habits that become a good part of their lives. Some of these habits affect the body, or the external self, while others support the mind and spirit, or the internal self. Our good habits may seem to be incidental, and often come to be taken for granted, but they are actually gifts we give to ourselves. And these gifts, when packaged together, become part of the system each of us uses to enhance our own life process. Some of the enhancers Judy and I have included in Superlife were stumbled upon; others were given to us by friends. In either case, they are a grab bag of gifts we can reach into on a daily basis to help us look and feel better.

DIET

Balance your diet to contain essential nutrients, vitamins and minerals in your daily fare, and consult a trained nutritionist for a specific diet suited to the requirements of your own individual system.

If you have been on a food binge and need to curtail "sloppy" eating (throwing everything into your mouth mindlessly), try one of the two radical, short-term diets given here. But consult your physician to be sure you can tolerate them even for the few days recommended.

SEVEN-DAY GRAPE FAST

For Seven Days: Select one variety of grape, one color only.

Eat grapes only for seven days, three times a day, as a replacement for breakfast, lunch and dinner.

Allow one pound of grapes for each of three meals daily (I sometimes taper off to less than a pound as I get into the fast and become adjusted to it).

Drink at least eight glasses of bottled water daily.

The only other beverage allowed is bottled, pure, red grape juice diluted with bottled water (two-thirds juice to one-third water).

Beverage Treat: Heat the grape-juice-and-water drink in a microwave oven or by other means. Drink it in a wineglass for a treat.

When coming off the fast, remember not to startle your system with the radical introduction of new, sharp foods. Instead, follow these instructions:

Eighth Day: Add other gentle fruits such as bananas and

apples; but avoid sharp, acidic fruits like oranges, grapefruit, and so on.

Ninth Day: Continue to eat the same fruits as on the eighth day; add other gentle juices, such as carrot juice or a "green (vegetable) drink," neither of which is acidic. No citrus juice is permitted.

Tenth Day: Add steamed vegetables—steamed so they retain their crunch; not raw but with the vitamins still intact.

Eleventh Day: Add your first protein since the fast by eating some low-fat cottage cheese. Keep eating steamed vegetables, fruits, gentle juices.

Add salads with a little lemon juice (these may also be added on the tenth day, in small amounts).

You may add other foods now, bearing in mind your own sense of their gentleness on your newly cleansed and refined digestive system.

SIX-DAY STEAK-AND-EGG DIET

First and Second Days:

Breakfast:	2 hard-boiled eggs
	Grapefruit juice, unsweetened
	Brewed or instant decaffeinated coffee or decaffeinated tea
Lunch:	1 pound of lean steak (the diet calls for a pound of steak, but you may not be able to eat that much; also, season the steak with a bit of pepper)
	Grapefruit juice
	Decaffeinated coffee or decaffeinated tea
Dinner:	2 hard-boiled eggs
	Grapefruit juice or dry white wine
	decaffeinated coffee or tea
Between meals:	Drink grapefruit juice or dry white wine

Third and Fourth Days: Breakfast, lunch and dinner: Surprise! You may eat anything you select, providing you think it is sensible to consume it on a diet geared to weight loss. If you prefer nonfatty fish, white-meat chicken with no skin, steamed vegetables, salads or fruits, have them. Just be sure you are using discipline so the foods you eat and the beverages you drink are not fattening and are consumed in the smallest possible amounts to satisfy you. Do not drink any alcohol during these two days except for dry white wine. Drinking grapefruit juice also helps during this time.

Fifth and Sixth Days: Follow the same regime as that of the first and second days.

Because this diet is designed to reduce retained excess fluid in the system, you will not find our customary recommended consumption of several glasses of water each day.

DRINKING WATER

Unless you are on the Steak-and-Egg Diet, drink six to eight glasses of water every day of your life. If your tap water is high in sodium or of poor quality, drink bottled water. (We prefer Evian from France, but we also like others not quite so expensive as that.) Do not drink the water with meals, and be sure, if it is bottled, that it is still, not bubbly. Regularly flushing your system with still, pure water is great for your health and helps you lose or maintain weight.

BATHING

The ideal is a hot—not scalding—bath in a tub, every day. Whenever you can take a hot tub bath, do it. Put your head back on the upper rim of the tub (with a rubber pillow if you have one), tilting your chin up a bit. Bend your knees slightly and do some key breathing, before and after you cleanse. If you prefer alternating with showers or have no tub, let the hot water run down your front and back in the key breathing, standing position: head back, shoulders and chest dropped, pelvis tilted forward and up, knees slightly bent. Key-breathe under the shower.

Scalding water is dangerous, but hot water, which melts away toxic energy, is the greatest natural relaxer when combined with good breathing.

EXFOLIATING YOUR BODY SKIN

Remove the top layer of dead cells from your body skin by using a loofah three times a week in the bath or shower.

Whether you have dry or oily skin, this permits the constant regeneration of new cells, which replace those that are dead or damaged by pollution. The loofah, used in the Orient for centuries, softens when soaked in water. Always apply a moisturizing body lotion after using it.

TO BOUNCE OR NOT TO BOUNCE

Many forms of exercise now enjoying popularity involve repeated bouncing, running or jogging on hard surfaces. Most

of the proponents of these types of exercise have been responsible in cautioning practitioners about possible back, leg and foot injuries and in explaining how to prevent them.

But we advise against bouncing up and down on hard surfaces for a different reason than injury. As people age, the force of gravity tends to pull down facial muscles as well as internal reproductive organs. The gravitational pull of slap, slap, slapping while you bounce on a hard surface during exercise increases the potential for sagging of facial skin and internal organs.

If you enjoy bouncing exercises (including jogging), try doing them on a mini-trampoline or rebounder. It can be used outdoors or in a small indoor space. We call ours "bouncebacks" because as we land, the resilient surface makes everything bounce right back up again.

FACIAL ENHANCERS

Try the following suggestions for clear, firm skin and reduction of facial stress:

THE BUF-PUF

The Buf-Puf works the same way for facial skin as the loofah does on body skin. Concentrate on using the gentler Buf-Puf, which is designed especially for the face, on and around the nose, mouth, upper lip, chin and between the eyebrows. Gentle scrubbing with a Buf-Puf removes dead cells, keeps pores clean and prevents the formation of blackheads and whiteheads. It also deters the growth of the small lines that tend to form on the upper lip, especially when women smoke. Follow using a Buf-Puf with a moisturizer.

CONTRACT YOUR FACIAL MUSCLES

Whenever you apply makeup, cleansers or creams to your face, contract the facial muscle in the area you are touching. This contraction keeps your face taut so that your fingers do not pull your skin this way and that, causing it to wrinkle, sag or become flabby.

When you feel tightness in the forehead, brows, cheeks, mouth or jaws, you are actually storing tension there. Learning to see that through the camera in my work has taught me to recognize it with the naked eye, as well. Do the following exercises for facial tension, and always start at the top to do a sequence.

EXERCISES FOR FACIAL TENSION OR STRESS

1. For the forehead: Press middle fingers against your forehead at points halfway down the forehead and approximately above the center of your eyes. As you apply pressure, pull fingertips in toward the center and do a key exhale. Repeat five times.

2. For the space between the brows: Place middle finger between your brows. As you apply pressure, do a prolonged exhale. Repeat five times.

3. For the brow area: Place two pads of thumbs under your brows. Apply pressure with thumb pads to tight area under your brows and do some key breathing. Start the pressure near your nose, then move thumbs to outside of your brows, applying pressure along the way. Do one sequence, from near the nose to the outside of your eyes. Repeat if desired.

(continued on next page)

4. For the cheeks: Using pads of both index fingers, apply pressure upward and inward directly under cheekbones. Key-breathe, exhaling as you apply pressure. Repeat five times.

5. For the upper lip: When we keep a lot of feelings inside, we often get exactly what the old expression says: a "stiff upper lip." To remove the tension, do a prolonged exhale as you raise your upper lip, scrunching it up as far toward your nose as possible. Repeat five times or more, as desired.

6. For the lower lip, tongue and throat: For tightness in this area, exhale deeply as you stick out your tongue. Keep your mouth open and stretch your tongue down as close to your chin as possible. Repeat five or more times.

7. For the jaw: Press hinges of your jaw at your cheekbones with your fingers. With that pressure applied, allow your jaw to fall wide open and relax. Be sure to do a key breathing exhale as you press the jaw hinges while jaw is dropping. Repeat five times.

THE SUN AND SKIN

By now, most of us have heard all the evidence. Ultraviolet rays from the sun can cause medical problems such as skin cancers and cosmetic ones such as premature aging. But none of us can completely avoid the sun, and many of us want to actually bask in it. If you tan easily, that does not mean you are exempt from the dangers of the sun. If you burn, swell and peel, you already know how dramatic the sun's effects can be. Either way, protect your facial and body skin by applying and reapplying products containing para-aminobenzoic acid (PABA) and sun protection factor (SPF). A lower SPF number indicates a product that merely screens some of the harmful ultraviolet rays; an SPF number of fifteen or more acts as a complete sun block. Always start your sun season with higher SPFs, and continue to use them on your face and other sensitive areas throughout the season. But if you should get burned, here are two things to do, depending on the severity of exposure:

1. **For dangerous sunburns:** Any sunburn that produces nausea, dizziness, immediate eruption of the skin surface or an actual fever requires instant attention from a doctor or hospital emergency facility. These may be second-degree or even third-degree burns requiring fast, professional medical treatment.

2. **For less severe sunburns:** Excessive body heat alternating with chills—along with stinging, red skin—usually signifies a sunburn you can treat at home. For this type of sun exposure, take two aspirin or other fever-reducing medication every four hours to stabilize the flip-flop of hot and cold sensations. Also soak Turkish towels in tepid water and apply them as compresses to all burned areas. When towels feel hot, let them cool in the room air (which is always cooler than your burned skin), then reapply them, resoaking the towels if they dry out. Repeat applications on all sunburned areas until you feel your body heat diminishing. Then apply a handful of water and moisturizing lotion (not cream—too sticky) to the treated areas. Drink lots of cool water and no alcohol. If you go out, take a light shawl to use in case you feel chilled, even in tropical climates. Take aspirin (if it's time to do that) and reapply compresses before bedtime for a more comfortable sleep.

OTHER WAYS TO USE KEY BREATHING

Here are a few additional effective uses for key breathing techniques:

1. Breathe into the cold: Under a cold blast from the shower or a cold rinse following a shampoo, exhale deeply. That will permit the cold to invigorate you without shocking your system or causing your body to hunch up from the impact. This same technique works if you are in an excessively cold climate, or otherwise feel chilled. It also succeeds in warming cold hands or feet. You may have "cold feet" as a sign of anxiety. Pulling up against that tension keeps your feet cold and causes you to retain anxiety in your neck and shoulders. Key exhales get the energy and heat in your blood moving again.

2. Breathe to relax a cramp or a muscle: Do some key breathing with deep exhales as you apply manual pressure to a cramp or a tight muscle. Exhale as you apply the fullest pressure. The pressure and exhale combine to cause expansion in an area that is probably being contracted in discomfort.

3. Breathe to offset tension headaches: Many friends tell us that key breathing helps headaches and sometimes prevents them. Relax and visualize the tension leaving your head as you breathe and exhale fully, or do this while simultaneously applying pressure to the aching area with your hands.

4. Breathe before certain medical procedures: Some medical procedures cause anxiety. Before having your teeth drilled, before a shot and before a vaginal examination, the entire body can become tense. This causes the procedure to be doubly uncomfortable. Key breathing dissolves that tension. Remember to exhale deeply just as the procedure begins; that is when the tension needs releasing most.

PREMENSTRUAL AND MENSTRUAL CARE

Many women speak of cramping, stress, backaches and overall discomfort caused by the menstrual cycle. If you suffer from any of these problems, here are a group of things you can do for relief:

1. **Replace depleted vitamins and minerals:** As menstruation can cause this depletion, supplement vitamins and minerals as follows:

Vitamin B₆—To decrease fluid buildup, take three fifty-milligram tablets one time each day during ovulation.

· **Calcium**—Take eight to ten calcium tablets daily, before and during menstruation, as a relaxant for muscles, nerves and organs.

· **Vitamin E**—Take eight hundred units daily, at one time. This helps utilize oxygen in the tissues and avoids tissue spasms which affect the function of ovaries and the uterus.

2. **Control your diet specifically:** Eat chicken and fish in place of red meat. Avoid processed or refined foods, especially sugar. Fruits are alkalizers and should be eaten no more than twice daily, as a high alkaline count makes us feel sluggish. Vegetables and vegetable juices are acidifying and, as they increase energy, can be consumed often at these times.

3. **Exercise:** Walking is excellent, helping to increase circulation through your pelvis and back. Swimming (unless in excessively cold water or climates) is good, too. Superlife joint rotations keep you from feeling stiff; stretches and balances tone and center you, and PKA Power Techniques renew your strength. Be sure to do Touching the Ceiling with Chin (abdominal sit-ups with a crossed leg) before the onset of your period. Your own intuition should guide you to the proper amount of activity for your system.

4. **Massage your lymph nodes:** To reduce swelling and soreness in your breasts, massage your lymph nodes twice a day for ten seconds each time. These lymph nodes are in the center of each armpit, against the ribs. They serve as a transportation system, carrying hormones and such fat-soluble vitamins as A and E to the body. They also carry waste from the tissues to the bloodstream for elimination.

5. **Use a pillow to relieve pressure in the pelvic girdle:** Lie on either right or left side, whichever you prefer. Bend your knees and pull them into your chest, keeping your top leg slightly higher to the chest. Put a pillow between your legs. You can sleep in this position or use it with key breathing for pressure relief.

6. **Key-breathe with a gentle pelvic slapping motion:** Key-breathe lying facedown on your bed. Flex your pelvis as you inhale, release it forward and up as you exhale. Do this repeatedly, making a gentle, slapping motion with your hips

during maximum discomfort. During menstruation, key breathing helps whether you are sitting, standing or lying, on your back or stomach. For maximum relief, exaggerate the last part of the exhale, tucking your pelvis way under and pushing it forward and upward.

COUNTERATTACKING ANXIETY, THE BLUES AND TRAVEL FATIGUE

If you find yourself feeling anxious, self-pitying, depressed or travel weary, here are some ways to effectively deal with or prevent those feelings.

Counterattack Against Anxiety: When an upcoming situation makes you anxious, ask yourself one question: "What's the worst thing that can happen?" Of course, with true danger or tragedy, the answer is often not encouraging. But most of us experience anxiety out of proportion to the reality of the situation. Often it is simply the unknown that we fear. Asking this one question of ourselves, along with some key breathing techniques, usually helps to put matters into the proper perspective.

Counterattack Against Self-pity: When you find yourself falling into a "blue funk" of self-pity, think of the ancient proverb: "I moaned because I had no shoes until I met a man who had no feet." It's fine to want more than you have, but it helps to see your desires or disappointments in perspective to others' lives, and this proverb is a great wrench for turning off the self-pity valve.

Counterattack Against Depression: The best thing we know of to end depression is to make yourself—even force yourself—do something for someone else. Severely depressed friends have told us that one of the most depressing aspects of their problem is the belief that the depression will never stop, even for a moment. Forcing yourself to do something for someone else does two things: It makes you think of the task and the other person; and while you perform the requirements of the task, you often find that depression has lifted to allow you to concentrate elsewhere. In that way, you show yourself that depression does stop, if even for minutes, and that you can do something about controlling it by assuming a responsibility.

Counterattack Against Travel Fatigue: First, try to be a wise traveler. Do not drink alcohol before or during a plane ride. The pressurization of airplane cabins causes dehydration, and dehydration weakens the body. Alcohol is a powerful dehydrating agent and increases fatigue from flying. Also, eat sparingly on a plane. Nibble at the meal, or just have the salad, or even bring a light snack from home. Eating a big meal while you're stuck in a small, movement-confining space for hours makes you exhausted. In addition, be sure to drink lots and lots of water while flying.

You can exercise by walking in the aisles, doing mini-stretches and joint rotations in your seat and while standing. (An empty galley or bathroom accessway is a great place to get the kinks out with subtle versions of Superlife exercises; you can stretch your feet in the front-, back- and side-kick positions, scaled down for space.) The same advice is true for long car rides, except that you can only do standing exercises when you stop for meals or gas. Whether you go by plane or car, do a full set of joint rotations and some stretches, as needed, when you reach your hotel or other destination.

BALLET

Being in a ballet class makes most of us feel beautiful. The movements are graceful and elegant, helping to create the feeling of beauty. In ballet, a great deal of emphasis is placed on pulling in your abdomen, tightening buttocks and pulling up your lower torso. Though those moves make the ballet stance so exquisite, they can also cause a tendency to continually contract the vaginal and sphincteral muscles when you are not in class. If you study ballet, be conscious of this tendency, and avoid it by doing some full key exhales during class (between exercises or routines) and afterward. This will help to release lower pelvic tension and contraction so that relaxation and sensitivity can be maintained in the pelvis.

LITTLE TREATS

You may have heard the expression: "When the going gets tough, the tough go shopping." Often even a new lipstick can do the trick. But here are two natural "uppers" we find ourselves using often.

Judy's "Water into Wine" Trick: Judy rarely has time for those long bathing/hair/makeup rituals when preparing for a business or social dinner appointment. Often she goes on to

dinner straight from the office, or has all of fifteen minutes at home or in a hotel room to prepare for the evening. As it's the hour when she feels tired anyway, a glass of wine would knock her out completely. But she always keeps a stemmed wineglass handy, fills it with cool bottled water and sips from it slowly. She does this while reapplying makeup. If she can, she also lies down, raises her feet higher than her head, sips from her wineglass and does three to five minutes of key breathing. It's like a minivacation—short but sweet.

Stefanie's Magic Pillowcase Trick: I own two or three exquisite pillowcases, acquired over the years. I often pack one of them in my limited travel luggage. At home or away—when I feel grungy, overworked or pressured—I put a special case on the pillow and apply some perfumed scent to the case. Relaxing against a scented pillowcase for a few minutes or throughout a night of sleep makes me feel I have escaped into a beautiful, comforting world.

LAUGHTER

Laughter . . . one of the great salvations of life! Laughter tempers pain, gives us a better perspective and relieves anxiety. Even when life seems very sane and serious, laughter reminds us of the absurdity that coexists with that sanity. Norman Cousins, in his book *Anatomy of an Illness*, tells us how laughter helped him survive a critical illness. Hospitals tell us there is a direct correlation between the ability to laugh and good health. Apart from being good for your mind and your spirit, laughter actually produces certain beneficial physical effects. When we laugh, our brains send out hormones that activate the release of endorphins, the body's natural painkillers. As in aerobics, our heart and blood rates rise when we laugh and drop below normal when we stop laughing; also, our muscles vibrate when we laugh, acting like a minimassage for bodily tension. There's a serious explanation as to why laughter feels so good! We always laughed a lot while filming "Hart to Hart," making the long hours of work seem like recreation. Laughter lets off steam, relaxes mind, body and spirit, makes your face look prettier and—best of all—makes life a lot more fun.

A FINAL THOUGHT FOR A SUPER LIFE

I have always been a social creature. So has Judy. Each of us is deeply aware that male and female family members, friends and coworkers bring special enrichments to our lives—enrichments that would not be possible in a solitary or isolated existence.

But we have also come to understand that too much dependency on our families or friends can be debilitating for everyone concerned. It can create unfair demands and expectations, misplaced trust and blame; and it can turn potentially happy, lifelong relationships into those that deteriorate with time and intimacy.

As with many other facts of life, this may appear to be a contradiction. Engaging in a relationship is surely an art. But as we have spoken a great deal about the art of personal well-being and the enhancement of one's own life process, we want to close by sharing with you a quote we particularly like. It is taken from the Zen book of wisdom known as the *Zenrin*, and asks the following question:

> If you do not get it from yourself,
> Where will you go for it?

THE CAST

Judy Quine

Bill Wallace

Ernie Reyes, Sr.

Ernie Reyes, Jr.